Buddhism
and
Mental Health

Harold G. Koenig, M.D.

DEDICATION

To my son Jordan

CONTENTS

ACKNOWLEDGMENT

For all the time and effort made by a precious colleague of mine, an
expert in Buddhism, who wrestled with me on many of the
controversial areas that are presented herein
(some of which could not be agreed on and the discussion continues)

INTRODUCTION

Buddhism is particularly relevant to mental health because Buddhist teachings often focus on the mind and development of the mind. Therefore, mental health professionals, chaplains, and pastoral counselors (particularly those who treat Buddhist clients) should be familiar with Buddhist beliefs/practices and their relationship to mental health.

Buddhism today is the world's fourth largest religion, with about 500 million adherents (7% of the world's population) (WCD, 2010). About 50% live in China and most of the remainder lives in Thailand (13%), Japan (9%), Burma/Myanmar (8%), and other countries of the Asia Pacific region (Pew Research Center, 2012a). The three branches of Buddhism today are Theravada, Mahayana, and Vajrayana.

Theravada Buddhism ('southern' Buddhism), the only sect that has survived in a continuous way since early times, has nearly 100 million adherents concentrated in Thailand (87% of the population is Buddhist), Burma/Myanmar (75%), Sri Lanka (69%), Laos (52%) and Cambodia (85%) (ARDA, 2016). This branch of Buddhism coexists with other religions in Southeast Asia such as Hinduism, Christianity, Islam, and folk religions. The scripture on which all branches of Buddhism are based, particularly Theravadin Buddhism, is the Pali Canon. The Pali Canon includes the ancient teachings and practices of Buddhism from the early centuries BCE (before the common era).

Mahayana Buddhism ('Eastern Buddhism') is the largest branch of Buddhism today. It is made up of an estimated 350 million adherents, most of whom reside in China (15% of population), Japan (56%), South Korea (25%) and Vietnam (49%) (ARDA, 2016). Similar to Theravada Buddhism, Mahayana Buddhism has coexisted in East Asia with many other endogenous religions such as Confucianism, Taoism, and Shintoism. Zen Buddhism is part of the Mahayana tradition.

The approximately 20 million adherents to *Vajrayana Buddhism* are concentrated mostly in Tibet (79% of the population), Nepal (12%), Bhutan (84%) and Mongolia (54%) (ARDA, 2016). Vajrayana Buddhism, sometimes called Tibetan Buddhism or 'northern' Buddhism, is also an offshoot of Mahayana Buddhism. The Dalai Lama is a member of this branch.

There has been growing interest in Buddhism in the United States, and with an increasing number of immigrants from Asian countries, Buddhists now make up approximately 0.07-1.9% of the U.S. adult population (based on estimates around the turn of the 21st century) (Wuthnow & Cadge, 2004). While Buddhists only make up a small percentage of the population, nearly one in eight Americans reports that Buddhist teachings or practices have had an important influence on their religion or spirituality. This is especially true for well-educated Americans (and those with well-educated parents), those living in the Northeast, non-Catholics, non-Evangelical Protestants, persons associated with the New Age movement, advocates of alternative medicine, individuals who have taken interreligious classes, and members of academic professions in the humanities and social sciences (Wuthnow & Cadge, 2004). Thus, mental health professionals in the U.S. who see patients with these demographics (or Asians) need to know something about Buddhism and its relationship to mental health.

In this small book, I first examine the person of the Buddha and the historical time period during which Buddhism arose. I then describe the beliefs and practices of Buddhists, and examine what Buddhists believe and practice today (based on original data collected from three national and cross-national datasets). Considering these Buddhist beliefs and practices, I then speculate on the relationship between religiosity and mental health, hypothesizing both positive and negative effects. To put these speculations to the test, I conduct a review of quantitative research on religiosity and mental health in Buddhists (along with a comparison of mental health in Buddhists and non-Buddhists). Both early research published prior to 2010 (based on a systematic review) is presented and recent research published during the past decade is described. As part of the latter, I present information based on an original analysis of worldwide datasets comparing the well-being of Buddhists and non-Buddhists and examining the relationship between religiosity and well-being in Buddhists. Finally, I make suggestions for mental health and religious professionals on how to apply this knowledge about Buddhist beliefs/practices and the findings from systematic research to the treatment of Buddhist clients.

The **primary audiences** for this book are mental health professionals and clergy who are called upon to help Buddhists deal with emotional and other mental health problems. However, given the careful attention to documentation, emphasis on research, and report of original research results, investigators who conduct studies in Buddhist populations, as well as healthcare systems that provide services to Buddhist clients, will also find this volume useful. Finally, lay Buddhists more generally will discover that the information contained here may be both enlightening and faith enhancing.

Please join me in this brief review of Buddhist teachings, objective examination of the relationship between Buddhism and mental health, and discussion of how this information can be integrated into the care of Buddhists that will not only address emotional problems but also strengthen faith and enhance the joy and meaning of life.

CHAPTER 1

THE BUDDHA

Buddhism arose out of an early Hindu culture in the 5th century BCE with the birth and teachings of Siddhartha Gautama (the Buddha or "awakened one"), a man who most scholars believe was a real person who lived near the Indian-Nepalese border.[1] Buddhism emerged around the time that the last of the Upanishads were written, a period when the Hindu ideal of renunciation of family and social life was becoming more and more widespread. Buddhism would become different from Hinduism in many ways, including a decreased emphasis on Hindu rituals (based on the Vedas) and Hindu deities. Perhaps the biggest difference, however, was a philosophical point. Hinduism focused on the "atman" (the self), which was viewed as a "wave" that is part of the ocean (the Self). In contrast, Buddhism emphasized the "anatta" or "anatman" or the "no self." The feeling that one has a "self" in Buddhism is viewed as a construction, similar

---

[1] Williams et al (2012, p 16) note that the relationship of the Buddha to Buddhism is quite different from the relationship of Jesus Christ to Christianity. The Buddha re-discovered the *sasana* or objective truth, which has always existed and will always exist whether individuals like the Buddha come or go. Christianity, in contrast, rests entirely on the birth, death, and resurrection of Jesus Christ.

to a dream and not reality. There are many discussions of this in the Pali Canon, such as the *Anattalakkhana Sutta* (found in the Samyutta Nikaya of the Pali Canon), which is chanted by many Buddhists.[1]

The Historical Buddha[2]

Gethin (1998) indicates that we know very little about the historical Buddha with any degree of certainty (which is also true for other religious leaders before and around the turn of the "common era" when written records first became available). What follows about the life of the Buddha below lies somewhere between historical fact and myth. Williams and colleagues (2012, p 21) describe the biography of the Buddha as a "hagiography," an idealizing account of the life of a saint or holy person that illustrates what is important to Buddhists (the Dharma) and what Buddhism is all about (i.e., a change in understanding that "would lead to seeing the way things really are in its fullest transformative sense, and thus to attaining liberation." Whether history, hagiography, or legend, the Buddha's story speaks of truths that transcend time.

According to tradition, Siddhartha (literally "he who achieves his aim") Gautama was the son of a local chieftain and grew up in a privileged and wealthy home (an important aristocratic family). After

---

[1] "Form, monks, is not self. If form were the self, this form would not lend itself to dis-ease. It would be possible [to say] with regard to form, 'Let this form be thus. Let this form not be thus.' But precisely because form is not self, form lends itself to dis-ease. And it is not possible [to say] with regard to form, 'Let this form be thus. Let this form not be thus.'

Feeling is not self...

Perception is not self...

[Mental] fabrications are not self...

Consciousness is not self. If consciousness were the self, this consciousness would not lend itself to dis-ease. It would be possible [to say] with regard to consciousness, 'Let my consciousness be thus. Let my consciousness not be thus.' But precisely because consciousness is not self, consciousness lends itself to dis-ease. And it is not possible [to say] with regard to consciousness, 'Let my consciousness be thus. Let my consciousness not be thus.'" (translated from the Pali by Thanissaro, 1993)

[2] Frequently cited in this section, and throughout the text more generally, are comments by **Paul Williams** (and colleagues), who is Professor of Indian and Tibetan Philosophy at the University of Bristol, England, and Theravada scholar **Rupert Gethin**, Professor of Buddhist Studies in the Department of Theology and Religious Studies and co-director of the Centre for Buddhist Studies at the University of Bristol, and president of the Pali Text Society.

examining him shortly after his birth, Brahmin specialists declared that he would be a great man someday, most likely a king. Wanting his son to pursue this career path, his father shielded him from religious teachings and any exposure to human suffering during his childhood and youth (Thaper, 2002, p 137). At the age of 16, he married his cousin (Yasodhara), who soon gave birth to a son (Rahula). For the next 13 years, prince Siddhartha lived with his family in luxury without want of material possession of any kind. However, as he neared the age of 30, he began to question his life:

"I was delicate, most delicate, supremely delicate. *Lotus* pools were made for me at my father's house solely for my use; in one blue lotuses flowered, in another white, and in another red. I used no sandal wood that was not from Benares. My turban, tunic, lower garments and cloak were all of Benares cloth. A white sunshade was held over me day and night so that I would not be troubled by cold or heat, dust or grit or dew ... Yet even while I possessed such fortune and luxury, I thought, 'When an unthinking, ordinary person who is himself subject to ageing, sickness, and death, who is not beyond ageing, sickness, and death, sees another who is old, sick or dead, he is shocked, disturbed, and disgusted, forgetting his own condition. I too am subject to ageing, sickness, and death, not beyond ageing, sickness, and death, and that I should see another who is old, sick or dead and be shocked, disturbed, and disgusted -this is not fitting.' As I reflected thus, the conceit of youth, health, and life entirely left me." (quoted from Gethin, 1998, pp 20-21)

He soon began to leave the palace regularly to see how the people in the surrounding community lived. What he saw during these outings confirmed his earlier ruminations. Everywhere he went Gautama found severe human suffering among the common people struggling to survive, poverty-stricken, dealing with painful illness, disability, old age, and inevitable death (Conze, 1959, pp 39-40; Gethin, 1998, p 21). All of this increased his distress, and made him realize that all pleasures in life were transitory, only temporarily covering up the suffering that pervaded all of life. There must be a solution to this suffering, and Siddhartha was determined to find it.

As a result, he renounced his normal role in society as husband

and father, left his wife, son, and family home, abandoned his future career as a leader and king, and went away to live as a wandering homeless ascetic begging for his food in the streets. His goal was to search for the truth that would ultimately lead to an end to suffering (his own and others). Soon after he left home, Siddhartha came under the tutelage of several Hindu teachers, learning the practice of yoga and meditation (Narada, 1992, pp 14-20). While what he learned here was important and useful, it was not enough for him. Siddhartha believed that there was more. So he sought Enlightenment through self-mortification and renunciation of food (reportedly eating only a single nut or leaf per day), eventually almost starving to death and drowning after he fell into a river because of his weak physical state. On recovery, he realized that asceticism was also not the answer.

Siddhartha then began to meditate (Conze, 1959, pp 47-51). After 49 days of meditation (at the age of 35), he reached a deep state of perfect equanimity and awareness (Jhana) where he awakened (bodhi) and attained Enlightenment. Although the time between the beginning of his search and enlightenment took only six years, the Buddha is thought to have lived many, many prior lives culminating in the present one. His past lives are described in the Jataka tales, which are part of the Pāli Canon (Khuddaka Nikaya of the Sutta Pitaka) (Babbitt, 2009).

Having reached Enlightenment, the Buddha taught what he had discovered about the cessation of suffering to everyone he could. He had realized that avoiding extremes of both self-indulgence and self-mortification (extreme asceticism) was the best way to achieve liberation from suffering. This way, known as the Noble Eightfold Path, was soon to be called the "Middle Way" (Thanissaro, 2010; Williams et al., 2012, p 21). The Buddha acquired more and more followers as he wandered along the banks of the Ganges, eventually forming a monastic order. The Buddha became viewed by followers as one who had achieved perfection in wisdom and compassion. They came to revere him and began to spread his message of hope that suffering could be ultimately done away with. By his death around the age of 80, the Buddha had acquired a large group of individuals, lay and monastic, dedicated to his teachings.

Speculations

The following musings are highly speculative, based on the present author's interpretation and limited understanding of Buddhism as a non-Buddhist scholar. The development of Buddhism from Hinduism is a topic of major scholarly interest and the discussion below may not do it justice. However, these thoughts provide a bridge to help explain why the Buddha eventually moved on from the Hindu religion of his day. That the Buddha moved on from Hinduism cannot be denied. Paul Williams, Professor of Indian and Tibetan Philosophy at the University of Bristol (England) says:

"The Buddha rejected the final religious authority directly, indirectly, or ideologically, of the social class of Brahmins in their primordial Scriptures, the Vedas, so important to Hinduism throughout history" (Williams et al., 2012, p 6).

How did the experiences of the Buddha before and after leaving his family influence his departure from Hinduism? This question is compelling because it may help to explain his departure from Hinduism and some of his later teachings.[1]

According to Gethin (p 20), Siddhartha as a young man had two destinies before him: become a great king or become a buddha. His father wanted very much for Siddhartha to pursue the former path. Consequently, he sheltered Siddhartha from "all things unpleasant and ugly such as old age, sickness, and death." This might have been to prevent his choosing a religious path rather than pursue the life of a leader or king. Although we certainly do not know for sure, this may have limited Siddhartha's understanding of the role that religious faith could play in the relief of suffering, since he may have had little exposure to either. After realizing the immense suffering that was the reality of the common people of his day, he first tried the religious path. Siddhartha sought training in yoga and was a student under several Hindu teachers, including Arada Kalama, a well-known hermit saint and teacher of yogic meditation, and Udaka Ramaputra,

---

[1] The comments that follow assume that the Buddha's story is historical. However, as noted above, if the Buddha's life story is more of a hagiography, one that illustrates the primary principles of Buddhism, then the psychological and social dynamics discussed here may be less relevant and so should be considered in that light.

8

a meditation teacher with a Brahmanical background. What he learned from them was helpful, but it was not enough. This may be why Siddhartha felt the need to go beyond Hindu teachings that emphasized the existence of God/Brahman and other deities, focusing instead on his own thoughts, mind and action – to reach a state of peace and tranquility, and once having achieved this, to teach it to others to relieve the suffering that he saw all around him.

A big question remained, though. The Buddha was certainly a remarkable man who had disciplined himself over years of intensive practice to control his mind through meditation. Was this way of living – the Eightfold Path – even possible for most of the people who lived during the Buddha's time? Not all the people of his day may have felt impoverished or distressed. However, there is no doubt that there were many who struggled to scrap together enough resources to survive. Did those who were not wandering ascetics and renouncers like the Buddha have *the time*, the circumstances, the self-discipline and fortitude to detach themselves from their relationships, possessions, pleasures, even their own selves, and engage in meditation that would lead them to that deep tranquil state? This way of living butted up against natural impulses, the biological makeup that motivates the human species. Most of the population had to work for a living, produce the food, the shelter, marry and have children, take care of their elders, and organize and protect the community against outside invaders seeking to take over their lands, homes, and few resources. Many could not even read and so did not have access to the Buddha's teachings, which were written down only hundreds of years after his death in different local languages.

Only a privileged few, then, had the time, ability, and motivation to pursue training as a monk, holy person, and disciple of the Buddha (bhikkhu or bhikkhuni). These individuals often left their homes, detached from their families, and went about begging for food since it took time and unhindered practice to strictly follow the Buddha's teachings. They were dependent on everybody else carrying out their roles (in work, family, and government). Otherwise, society could not function. In Hinduism, the Bhagavad Gita around the same time proposed a compromise that involved an emphasis on activity, work, and doing one's duty (as assigned by their caste), while detaching oneself from the results of these efforts (Johnson, 1994). Without the hope of reward, pleasure and success at the end of the day, however, what would keep people motivated to do the hard work that needed to be done? This is probably why the caste system was so important in India at this time. Everyone had their role, and it was imperative that they follow that role for society to function. There were the *brahmanas* (and later bhikkhus) who were considered holy men, ascetics, those who had the time to meditate, study the Vedas or the Buddha's teachings. Next, there was the *ksatriyas* -- the ruling class and warriors who organized and protected the community. Then there were the *vaisyas* – the farmers, builders, and merchants who provided the food and the shelter. Finally, there were the *sudras* – the workers who took care of the fields, the business, and the households. This system functioned well as long as everyone did what they were supposed to, which was determined by the family into which they were born. Thus, the Buddha's solution to the suffering he had observed among the common people of his day was really available only to one particular class of citizens, the wandering renouncers who were supported by the masses around them and had time on their hands.

Interestingly, Gethin (1998) indicates that the largest branch of Buddhism today, Mahayana Buddhism, may have begun as a "popular religious protest against the elitist monasticism of early Buddhism" (p 4). While he refutes this view by noting that Mahayana Buddhism actually began as a minority monastic sect, it is clear that 'mainstream' Buddhism was far from monastic in the way it developed for most Buddhist lay persons – particularly those in the Mahayana tradition.

The speculations above need to be tempered in light of what some experts in Buddhism have stressed in their writings. First, from the earliest known times, the Pali Canon sutras and historical documents describe followers of the Buddha that included laymen and laywomen. For example, there are many sutras in the Pali Canon in which the Buddha teaches lay people (Bodhi, 2005), a point also underscored in the writings about the Buddhist emperor Ashoka (Nikam & McKeon, 1978). Second, while it is true that not everyone could lead the life of a renunciate monk or nun, following the Eightfold Path did not require becoming a monk or nun. Indeed, it was a teaching for all Buddhists, monastics or lay. In other words, those in monastic orders may have become a "privileged class" but it was not necessary to be a monastic to be a Buddhist. Buddhists could be of any caste or class. Whether they had the time and the discipline to follow the Path, though, remains an issue. Thus, this is a complex subject which requires more space than available here to fully discuss.

For now, however, as I begin to examine Buddhist beliefs and practices, it is important to differentiate what Buddhist monks, scholars and theologians say Buddhists should believe and do from what Buddhist laypersons today actually believe and do in real life (admittedly, a challenge faced by the followers of Christianity and other major world religions as well). The way Buddhists believe and practice varies depending on region of the world and the extent to which core Buddhist beliefs have been integrated with local religious, cultural, and family or community traditions, handed down from generation to generation (see research on Buddhism in Asians, Chapter 4). Many of the Buddhist beliefs and practices described below are strictly practiced primarily by monks, nuns, or dedicated laypersons with the resources, education, and time to study, meditate, and think about such things. Nevertheless, the ethical values, wisdom, and meditative practices taught by the Buddha have had a tremendous influence on Buddhists of all traditions and time periods (many of whom may have not read a single word of any of the Buddhist canonical scriptures).

Conclusions
The Buddha, whether historical or not, was the individual responsible for the emergence of Buddhism from Hinduism in India during the 5th century BCE. The story of his life illustrates what is important to Buddhists (the Dharma) and what Buddhism is all about (i.e., the renunciation of the world leading to a view of reality as it truly is and therefore a transformation that produces liberation from suffering.

CHAPTER 2

BUDDHIST BELIEFS AND PRACTICES

Many Buddhist beliefs and practices are described in the Buddhist scriptures (see **Figure 1**), writings that were often composed of the "sayings of the Buddha" as recorded by his followers. The volume of these scriptures is estimated to be 1000 times the content of the Bible. These are called *buddhavacana* or "word of the Buddha" and are referred to as *sutras* (in Sanskrit) or *suttas* (in Pali). The texts which Buddhists consider to be sacred (or 'the canon') vary depending on the particular branch of Buddhism.

In Theravada Buddhism, the Pali Canon or Tripitaka contains the sayings that have been accorded to the Buddha and are the earliest recorded (agreed on during the 1st Buddhist Council in 404 BCE, but not written down until the 4th Buddhist Council around 29 BCE). Tripitaka means "three baskets" and reflects three sections of suttas: the Sutta Pitaka, the Vinaya Pitaka, and the Abhidhamma Pitaka. The first two were viewed as sayings of the Buddha, whereas the last one (Abhidhamma) is attributed to the Buddha, but was agreed on later.

An important Buddhist text from the Pali Canon is the Dhammapada ("Treasury of Truth"). This relatively short volume is a collection of sayings from the Buddha on moral and philosophical teachings. It makes up only a tiny fraction of the total Buddhist scriptures, but is perhaps one of the most widely read. The Dhammapada comes from the Khuddaka Nikaya portion of the Pali Canon (last portion of the Sutta Pitaka).

The scriptures of Mahayana Buddhism include additional sutras that are not found in the Pali Canon. The Mahayana sutras are as important as those in the Pali Canon, and so cannot be ignored. For example, there is the Chinese Buddhist canon (or Taishō Tripiṭaka or a-ts'ang-ching) of sutras recorded in the early centuries CE. While Mahayana Buddhists consider the Pali Canon as sacred, they revere these additional Mahayana sutras (sayings of the Buddha) as distinctive in their own right. The Lotus Sutra and Heart Sutra are examples of sutras that are particularly important to many Mahayana Buddhists. Vajrayana Buddhism branch of Mahayana Buddhism has additional scriptures special to Vajrayana Buddhists. As noted for Mahayana Buddhists, Vajrayana Buddhists consider the Pali Canon as sacred along with their own scriptures.

Note that the Buddha's teachings were passed down from generation to generation through his disciples by word of mouth and were not written down until hundreds of years later (nearly 400 years after the Buddha's death). It is likely, then, that the sacred Buddhist texts available today include both the words of the Buddha and those of his followers who passed down his words (De Jong, 1993).

Buddhist Beliefs

Although beliefs vary in Buddhism, a core belief common to almost all Buddhists involves "taking refuge" in the Buddha (the model), the Dhamma (teachings of the Buddha, i.e., the law/truth), and the Sangha (followers of the Buddha, consisting of laypersons, monks or nuns) (Dhammapada 190).[1] These are called the Three Jewels of Buddhism. Taking comfort or refuge in anything else, then, is contrary to Buddhist beliefs and therefore represents a false refuge or at least a refuge that is not secure (Dhammapada 188-189).

---

[1] All citations and quotes from the Dhammapada are taken from: Carter JR, Palihawadana M (2000). *The Dhammapada: The Sayings of the Buddha* (Oxford World's Classics). Oxford, UK: Oxford University Press

Figure 1. Historical timeline for Buddhism

Siddhartha Gautama (The Buddha)
(circa 567-484 BCE)

1st Buddhist Council
(sayings of Buddha agreed upon)
Sutta Pitaka, Vinaya Pitaka
(404 BCE)

Abhidhamma Pitaka
(circa 300 BCE)

Theravada Buddhism
(emerges in 200-300 BCE)
(Burma, Cambodia, Laos, Thailand and Sri Lanka)

Pali Tipitaka or Pali Canon
(Sutta Pitaka, Vinaya Pitaka, Abhidhamma Pitaka)
(written down 29 BCE during 4th Buddhist Council)

Minor Collection
Khuddaka Nikāya, part of the Sutta Pitaka, includes Dhammapada

Mahayana Tradition
(emerges in 100-200 CE)
(China, Japan, Korea, Vietnam)
Mahayana Sutras (Lotus and Wisdom sutras being most important)
Chinese Tripitaka

Vajrayana Buddhism
(emerges out of Mahayana Buddhism 400-600 CE)
(Tibet, India, Nepal, Bhutan, Mongolia)
Vajrayana tantras (600-700 CE)
Tibetan Canon (1300-1400 CE)

Sources. Carter & Palihawadana, 2000; Buddhism, 2015 and 2016; Flesher, 2016; Buddhist Society, 2016 (dates are approximate, and the Buddha's death may have been closer to 400 BCE than 500 BCE, according to Williams et al., 2012)

The Four Noble Truths represent the core of Buddhist doctrine (Dhammapada 273), and are reported to be his first teachings after having reached Enlightenment (Woodward, 1973). They are particularly important because they describe *how* craving results in suffering. The Four Noble Truths are:

1. *Life is dukkha* (suffering, pain, dissatisfaction, misery, lack of perfection). This includes being separated from loved ones and being attached to those who do not love in return. The realizing of dukkha prompts a person to action. The Buddha illustrated this realization by comparing it to someone who discovers his or her hair is on fire (Rhys Davids, 1971), requiring immediate action to put it out. This is how the must have Buddha felt when leaving his parental home, where he was protected and all needs provided, and then suddenly discovering that there was tremendous suffering in the surrounding community.

2. *The cause of suffering is craving*, i.e., desire for what one does not have. Craving arises from dependence on one's feelings or emotions (*vedana*), which may be enjoyable, unpleasant, or neutral. The focus of craving may be (a) pleasurable experiences from food, sex, or drugs/alcohol; (b) a particular state of mind (looking forward to being with a loved one, going on a vacation, or having a pleasant experience); or (c) a desire to avoid unpleasant feelings.

3. **The cessation of suffering** is possible, i.e., that freedom, liberation from suffering is achievable. Cessation of suffering depends on the *cessation of craving*, the liberation from attachments of every kind. Cessation of suffering is achieved when one reaches Enlightenment or Nirvana – the true "refuge" from all suffering. The belief that such a state exists, that it can be reached, and the powerful yearning that results from it is called *sraddha*. Sraddha is often translated as "faith" (often related to faith in the Dhamma), which is different from the way the term faith is used in Western religions and in Christianity particularly, where faith means belief and trust in a personal God (although see below discussion of how the Dhamma may in some respects represent God).

4. **The way leading to cessation of suffering** is the *Eightfold Path* (Dhammapada 273-289). The Eightfold Path involves seeking right understanding, right intention, right action, right speech, right livelihood, right effort, right mindfulness, and right concentration.

1. ***Right understanding*** (*samma ditti*) is the ability to distinguish wrong views (those that do not lead to Enlightenment) from right views (those that do). For example, a wrong view is that suffering can be escaped and lasting happiness can be achieved here through relationships, occupation, or any other activity (i.e., seeking a false refuge because of "ignorance"). A right view is that everything is subject to change and nothing is permanent, including the self, ego, or soul. Buddhists do not believe in "sin," but rather emphasize that ignorance is to blame, which encourages a sense of compassion for those who are behaving badly.

2. ***Right intention*** (*samma sankappa*) involves motivation, purpose in life, and inclinations that naturally follow from right understanding. This involves a desire to renounce attachments, stop clinging to pleasure, wealth, power and fame, and to avoid hatred, all violence or cruelty resulting from unrestrained greed.

3. ***Right action*** (*samma kammanta*) involves a set of behaviors that are proscribed and a set that are prescribed. Proscribed are killing of any living beings, including animals, whereas prescribed behavior is compassion on all. Proscribed are cheating, stealing, or otherwise gaining possessions by dishonest means, whereas prescribed behavior is respect of others and their possessions. Proscribed is sexual misconduct such as adultery, rape, and other illicit sexual behaviors, whereas prescribed behavior is to show respect for others.

4. ***Right speech*** (*samma vacha*) involves no lying, gossip, saying bad things about others (slander), or crude talk. Right speech is speaking softly, gently, affectionately, while avoiding angry, bitter, harsh or divisive speech. Right speech promotes peace and harmony between others.

5. ***Right livelihood*** (*samma ajiva*) means the avoidance of any occupation that may involve harm to others or contribute to their suffering. This might involve dealing in weapons or arms, drugs or intoxicants, slave trafficking, prostitution, or trickery of any kind (including high pressure sales). Originally (for monastics), it meant seeking to possess only what was essential to sustain life, which often meant begging for food.

These first five paths (understanding, intention, action, speech, and livelihood) focus on the wisdom and ethics of Buddhism, sometimes called the "five moral precepts," and are the foundation on which the last three paths (involving mindfulness and meditation) rest. The 10 "'perfections" are derived from the first five paths: generosity, morality, vigor, wisdom, patience, truthfulness, resolve, loving kindness, equanimity, and without desire. The perfections are said to lead one to the awakened state if practiced diligently (as done by the Buddha in his past life immediately prior to his present one) (Gethin, 1998, p 18). The last three steps of the Eightfold Path deal with meditation, concentration, and control of the mind.

6. ***Right effort*** (*samma vayama*) means that people can change by personal effort, i.e., change the unwholesome states in their lives and increase or adopt wholesome states. This includes stopping whatever thoughts or actions stand in the way of ethical or compassionate behavior, and letting go of greed, fear, hatred, or other negative mind states, especially guarding against unwholesome thoughts that might disrupt meditation or mindfulness. Effort like this is required to retrain the mind for effective meditation (below).

7. ***Right mindfulness*** (*samma sati*) includes constantly paying attention to whatever is happening in the present moment, including one's actions. Right mindfulness keeps the mind in the present moment, rather than allowing wandering thoughts about the past or the future to interrupt. One purpose of remaining present-focused and being open to whatever arises is so that right views can guide activity and right efforts can be made to accomplish daily tasks. This is done when brushing one's teeth, showering, and eating, as well as while working on the job and relating to co-workers, friends, and family.

8. **Right concentration** (*samma samadhi*) involves focusing on a single object and excluding everything else (in contrast to mindfulness). The goal is to unify the mind and bring conscious attention to a single point. This practice helps to train the mind and quiet the thoughts, leading to deep states of awareness and tranquility. In Buddhism, the path to peace and tranquility is through eight stages of meditation or *Jhana*: four form (*rupa*) and four formless (*arupa*) meditations leading to one-pointedness.

The Dhamma, the teachings of the Buddha (which includes the Four Noble Truths and Eightfold Path), is an essential concept in Buddhism (perhaps "the" essential concept). Williams and colleagues (2012, p. 6) quote Buddhist theologian Narada Thera as saying, "The original Pali term for Buddhism is *Dhamma*...Dhamma is that which really is. It is the doctrine of reality. It is a means of deliverance from suffering and deliverance itself. Whether the Buddhas arise or not, the Dhamma exists from all eternity."

Buddhists, then, believe that the Dhamma is the ultimate truth and is *the way* of achieving liberation or reaching nirvana, the primary goal of Buddhism. Buddhists believe that the Dhamma is the absolute objective truth. In fact, Williams et al (2012, p 6) go on to say that "In using 'Dharma' for his teaching the Buddha intentionally chose a term which was intended to indicate to others that he truly knew and taught how things finally are. Where others disagree, they do not have the Dharma. What they teach is in that respect its negation, Adharma." Thus, Buddhism (while often existing with other religions) is strictly speaking an exclusive religion, i.e., it excludes other paths to the truth and to ultimate reality. Thus, Buddhist beliefs would conflict with those of religions such as Christianity, another exclusive religion, where Jesus claims "I am the way and the truth and the life. No one comes to the Father except through me" (John 14:6).

Admittedly, not all Buddhist scholars would agree to what I have written above, i.e., about the exclusivity or elitism of Buddhism (furthermore, many Christian scholars would not agree that Christianity is exclusive). Some would argue that the Dhamma or Dharma[1] is a topic that is very complicated, and that there are many

---

[1]"Dhamma" in Pali, "Dharma" in Sanskrit

different yet valid ways to discuss this sacred concept in Buddhism (for insights in this regard, see the glossary of terms, Insight Meditation Society, 2017). For example, there is a quote from Thich Nhat Hanh (1999a) in his classic entry book into Buddhism where he says, "Whenever the Four Noble Truths and Noble Eightfold Path are practiced, the living Dharma is there. There are said to be 84,000 Dharma doors...To take refuge in the Dharma is to choose the doors that are most appropriate for us" (p 164). Elsewhere Hanh notes, "The Buddha respected people's desire to practice their own faith, so that is why he encouraged the Brahman man in his own language.[1] If you enjoy walking meditation, practice walking meditation. If you enjoy sitting meditation, practice sitting meditation. But preserve your Jewish, Christian, or Muslim roots. That is the best way to realize the Buddha's spirit. If you are cut off from your roots, you cannot be happy" (p 169). Thus, whether Buddhism in exclusive or inclusive will depend to some extent on who you read.

Buddhist Cosmology

Besides the Four Noble Truths and Eightfold Path, there are also Buddhist beliefs about how the world and universe are constructed. There is no creator or first cause according to "standard" Buddhist doctrine. As in Hinduism, Buddhists usually believe in reincarnation.[2] Reincarnation involves a beginning-less and endless series of birth, life, death and rebirth (*samsara*) that a person seeks to escape from (*moksha*) in order to reach *nirvana*. Nirvana represents a transcendent state free from enslaving bonds where suffering is gone and is characterized by profound peace and wisdom. Buddhists believe that the quality of each rebirth depends on a person's *karma* or actions during past lives. There is rarely memory of prior lives, except perhaps among children. However, this varies depending on

---

[1] This is in reference to an earlier discussion described by Hanh between the Buddha and a Brahman who asked him "What can I do to be sure that I will be with Brahma after I die?" The Buddha's reply was "As Brahma is the source of Love, to dwell with him you must practice the 'Brahma Abodes,' (*Brahmaviharas*) or Four Immeasurable Minds – love, compassion, joy, and equanimity" (p 169)

[2] Belief in reincarnation is not necessarily required in Buddhism, and some Buddhists think of reincarnation only in metaphorical interpretations. However, the whole purpose of the Dhamma (the teachings of the Buddha) is liberation from the cycle of birth and re-death, which involves reincarnation.

Buddhist tradition. For example, in the Tibetan tradition the Dali Lama had to be tested as a child for memory of his past life. Memory of past lives is also an attribute of a Buddha.

With regard to *karma*, the Buddha is reported to have given the following response to someone who asked him why there was such a variety in people's life situations (healthy, sick, poor, rich, ugly, beautiful, fortunate, unfortunate, etc.): "All living beings have actions (Karma) as their own, their inheritance, their congenital cause, their kinsman, their refuge. It is Karma that differentiates beings into low and high states" (Sayadaw, n.d.).

According to Buddhist cosmology, there are six realms of existence that humans may go through in the un-awakened state that range from (1) hell (naraka-gati) to (2) hungry ghost (preta-gati) (consumed by getting things in life, sometimes portrayed as a famished person with a tiny mouth) to (3) animal (tiryagyoni-gati) (all different life forms) to (4) human (manusya-gati)[1] to (5) demi-god or titan (asura-gati) (formless spirits detached from the world) to (6) god (deva-gati) realm. In the final god (deva) realm, one is born into the world into a wealthy, successful family, where the person has all their wants and desires fulfilled (as in the case of the Buddha). This final stage may involve a period prior to birth when one exists in "the heaven of the contented" (tusita), when one becomes a Bodhisattva (Gethin, 1998, pp 17-18). The belief is that a Bodhisattva will be reborn into the world to become a buddha when times are difficult and people need guidance on how to live (i.e., need a savior of sorts).

However, when a person is reborn into the god/deva realm, this does not guarantee Enlightenment or a final release (moksha), since motivation at this stage may not be very strong because all of one's material needs are being met. This could hinder the person from reaching the selfless, unattached state and ultimate release. Nevertheless, suffering is difficult to escape even in the best of circumstances, and disillusionment soon follows after all earthly desires have been fulfilled, as the early life of the Buddha illustrates.

Sansara (circle of death and rebirth) raises the question of what exactly is reborn. In Hinduism, there is belief that the soul or mind or consciousness or something transcendent (atman) is that which is

---

[1] Note that the best realm in which to be born in order to become enlightened is the human realm, where there is experience of suffering along with sufficient good conditions to be able to follow the Path.

reborn during the samsara cycle. However, given the Buddha's early teachings about the doctrine of "no self" or *anatta* (i.e., no such thing as a self or an unchanging, permanent soul), this created a problem for Buddhists with belief in the cycle of death and rebirth since there had to be some kind of continuity between the entity that was reborn and accumulated karma from previous lives. Buddhist scholars from the Theravada tradition later began to teach that there was a type of continuity of the self in the same way that "a flame is transferred from one candle to another" or like being a wave in the ocean but not part of current (see Kalupahana 1975). According to some experts, the Buddha never said that there was no self or soul, but emphasized that the question itself was misguided, emphasizing that one should focus on avoiding any attachment to the self or ego, which causes suffering (Thanissaro, 1996). Says Williams et al (2012, p. 24):

> "I agree with Gombrich elsewhere, where he considers the possibility held by some scholars that the Buddha may really have taught a Self (atman; Pali: atta) instead of the not-Self (anatman; Pali: anatta) doctrine. He observes, 'I myself find this claim that on so essential a point the Buddha has been misunderstood by all his follower somewhat [to use a Buddhist expression] 'against the current' (Gombrich 1971:72 n. 18)."

The explanation of anatta, then, varies depending on the particular branch of Buddhism and expert that one consults.

This raises another interesting question. What happened to the Buddha after he died? Do traditional Buddhists believe that he simply became non-existent? According to Theravada scholar Rupert Gethin (1998, p. 28), the answer to that question presents a problem and so is somewhat vague:

> "If we say that the Buddha exists, then the round of rebirth continues for the Buddha and the quest for an end to suffering has not been completed. On the other hand, to say that the Buddha simply does not exist is to suggest that the Buddhist quest for happiness amounts to nothing but the destruction of the individual being-something which is specifically denied in the

texts. Hence the strict doctrinal formulation of Buddhist texts is this: one cannot say that the Buddha exists after death, one cannot say that he does not exist, one cannot say that he both exists and does not exist, and one cannot say that he neither exists nor does not exist."

These considerations, then, raise questions about the impermanence of the self in Buddhism, and whether or not there is a place for God in this belief system (which I will address in the next chapter).

Buddhist Practices

Buddhism is primarily about action and intention (Williams et al., 2012, p. 26). Meditation is one of the primary ways by which Buddhists bring about change and movement towards Enlightenment, a state characterized by seven factors: mindfulness, investigation of dhamma, energy, rapture, tranquility, concentration or integration of mind, and equanimity (Carter and Palihawadana 2000, p 74). Among the major types of Buddhist meditation are samatha (common to all Indian religions, where the aim is to focus the mind on a single point and thereby reach a calm state), vipassana (insight meditation), and satipatthana (mindfulness meditation), anapanasati (focus on breath). There are also many other forms. Yet, today, meditation remains an uncommon practice among the majority of Buddhists outside the U.S. The self-discipline necessary to train the mind to focus and not wander is monumental (there is an unsubstantiated rumor that the reason tea became so popular in China was that it helped prevent those trying to meditate from falling asleep). Even among Asian Buddhists in the U.S. (where lack of time due to survival needs is less of an issue), 60% seldom or never meditate and only 14% meditate every day, which is even less frequent than Asian Christians in the U.S. meditate (24%) (Pew Research Center, 2012b).

The same is true for Buddhists worldwide outside of the U.S. (Lewis, 2012). In Thailand, where 87% of the population is Buddhist, meditation is primarily taught in monasteries. While there are reportedly 33,000 monasteries in Thailand, the percentage of Thai who meditate has not been reported (Cooke, 2010). One study of 3,100 patients with cancer in Japan found that of the 44.6% who used some form of complementary and alternative medicine (CAM),

3.8% (n=53) used Qigong (which includes meditation as a component) (Hyodo et al., 2005). This finding is consistent with an Internet-based study of 30,665 adults in Japan of whom 3.9% practiced meditation (Shiba et al., 2015). In a random sample of 468 adults (31% Buddhist, 11% Tao, 7% Hindu, 17% Christian, 16% Islam, 19% Free Thinker) in Singapore, 76% used some form of CAM: 2.1% practiced Tai Ji or Qigong and 1.8% practiced Ayurveda or yoga (Lim et al., 2005). In another study of CAM practices in Singapore that involved a consecutive series of 65 cancer patients receiving radiation therapy at Singapore's National Cancer Institute, only 3% of participants practiced meditation (Wong et al., 2010). Finally, in a study of CAM practices among 222 rheumatology patients in Seoul, Korea, 2% said they used religious or spiritual interventions (Kim & Seo, 2003). The frequency of the meditation reported in these studies of East Asians is far below the 8% of Americans who practice meditation as part of CAM (Clarke et al., 2015).

Other Practices

Buddhist practices that involve "taking refuge" may involve the practice of rituals in a temple (institutionalized) or at home. Many Buddhists may have a small shrine in their home that often includes a picture or statue of the Buddha, to which they make offerings of clean water, flowers or incense. This shows gratitude and respect for the Buddha and his teachings. This practice, however, depends on the particular country, branch of Buddhism, family tradition, and education level. At least in theory, Buddhist practices that involve prayer and meditation either in the community temple or in the home are not transactional like in the West, i.e., they are not typically done in order to "get something." However, these worship practices are thought to have consequences in terms of karma that will ultimately benefit the person.

Buddhist Clergy

Buddhist teachers can be monastics or laypersons. Buddhist monks are male and Buddhist nuns are female (originally called bhikkhu and bhikkhunis). Buddhist monks and nuns practice renunciation and celibacy. In some countries such as Japan and Korea, some Buddhist monks (called 'priests') have taken on administrative duties including performing worship services and temple rituals, and other tasks such as registering births, marriages, and deaths. They may also be employed in a secular job in the community, and be either celibate or married. Buddhist holy men and women lead an austere lifestyle, are often in their later years (final stages of renunciation), and are considered sages and teachers. They may live in a monastery or temple, although for a time may have also lived in the mountains or forests (at least during early Buddhism). The Dhammapada says this about the followers of the Buddha:

> "Not for this is one a bhikkhu, merely that one begs of others; having taken up a gross dhamma, one is not thereby a bhikkhu. Setting aside both merit and wrong who lives here the higher life, courses in the world discriminately, he, indeed, is called 'bhikku.' One does not become a sage by silence, if confused and ignorant. But a wise one, as if holding a set of scales, takes up the best, and shuns wrongs, he is a sage" (266-269).

Conclusions

The most widely known sacred Buddhist text is the Pali Canon (Tripitaka), although the Dhammapada may be the scripture that is most widely read by Buddhists. The Pali Canon is particularly revered by Theravada Buddhists, although this is also true to some extent for Mahayana and Vajrayana Buddhists (although they have their own sacred texts). The core Buddhist belief across all traditions is "taking refuge" in the Buddha, the Dhamma, and the Sangha. Soon after Enlightenment, the Buddha began to teach the Four Noble Truths, with the fourth Truth describing the Eightfold Path on how to achieve liberation from samsara (the endless cycle of death and rebirth) and reach nirvana (cessation of suffering). Buddhist cosmology involves several states of existence of the un-awakened person, progressing through six stages from lower to higher states. The Buddha's early teachings involved the doctrine of "no self," which helped to distinguish Buddhism from Hinduism. However, this doctrine raises questions about what entity is being reborn and accumulating karma, as well as whether the Buddha continues to exist in some state after his death, issues which Buddhist scholars wrestle with. Concerning Buddhist practices, meditation is central to the last three steps of the Eightfold Path, although appears to be an infrequent practice among Asian Buddhists. More common are the practice of rituals that takes place either in Buddhist temples or at home, where a small shrine may be set up that includes a picture or statue of the Buddha, to which Buddhists make offerings as a show of gratitude and respect.

CHAPTER 3

BUDDHISM AND GOD

As the reader may have gathered from the last chapter, the teachings of the Buddha in the sutras are more about a philosophy of how to live life, than a religion that involves deities or supernatural entities. Classic Buddhism is considered a non-theistic religion because it does not promote belief in God as a distinct and discrete being with personal attributes as Western theistic religions view God (Thera, 2004) or as Hindus might do so (Knapp, 2016). When asked about a Supreme Being, the Buddha reportedly either remained silent or discouraged such questions (Jayaram 2016), as when he was asked about the "self." Ambedkar (1957) reports a conversation between a religious man and the Buddha that addresses this issue. Although the Buddha did not explicitly rule out the existence of God (whom he acknowledges as 'the Absolute') during that conversation, he argued *against* the notion that either the Absolute or Ishavara (God as understood by Hindus as a person) was the creator. He stated that our deeds are the creator of good or evil, concluding the discussion with this statement:

> "Let us, then, surrender the heresies of worshipping Ishavara and praying to him; let us not lose ourselves in vain speculations of profitless subtleties; let us surrender self and all selfishness; and as all things are fixed by causation, let us practice good so that good may result from our actions."

Gethin (1998, p. 65) also emphasizes that Buddhists do not believe in a creator God, as do Williams et al (2012, p. 3) who say: "Buddhists have no objection to the existence of the Hindu gods, although they deny completely the existence of God as spoken of in e.g. orthodox Christianity, understood as the omnipotent, omniscient, all-good, and primordially existent creator deity, who can be thought of as in some sense a person" (a statement repeated by these authors a second time on p. 5). However, since the Buddha only traveled about 200 miles from his home during his lifetime, he may not have been aware of the monotheistic Abrahamic tradition of the Jews. As noted earlier, though, he did have a generally negative view towards the Hindu religion as practiced during his lifetime:

> "Many for refuge go to mountains and to forests, to shrines that are groves or trees - humans who are threatened by fear.
> This is not a refuge secure, this refuge is not the highest. Having come to this refuge, one is not released from all misery."
> (Dhammapada 188-189)[1]

The Buddha wanted his followers to avoid the distractions brought on by theological speculations about God or gods, and instead focus on right living and virtuous actions that would lead to the relief of suffering.

While most Buddhists in the Theravada branch do not emphasize deities of any sort, this is not always the case for other Buddhist traditions. For example, when Buddhism spread to various places in the East and mixed with local religions, a number of cultures included a devotional element to Buddhism (Encyclopedia Britannica, 2004). This was especially true for Mahayana Buddhism, but also to some extent for Vajrayana Buddhism. For example, in Mahayana Buddhism there is belief in bodhisattvas or compassionate beings that exist in the highest level of existence and serve to guard the world and come into the world to alleviate suffering. Mahayana Buddhists consider the Buddha to be an embodiment of the "cosmic dharmakāya," which has been described as "the body of reality itself,

---

[1] Some might disagree that this quote refers to the Hindu religious practices. If about nature spirits, then this may be different from standard Hindu belief or practice of the time.

without specific, delimited form, wherein the Buddha is identified with the spiritually charged nature of everything that is" (Ray, 2001). The cosmic dharmakaya, then, resembles the notion of God (or at least Brahman in a pantheistic sense as taught in Hinduism).

Some Mahayana Buddhists may honor, pray to, and worship a divine-like being called Avalokiteśvara (translated literally "Lord who looks down"). Avalokiteśvara is a bodhisattva who embodies mercy, compassion, kindness and love. Despite being able to reach nirvana, Avalokitesvara delays doing so in order to help humans on earth who are suffering (Leighton 1998). Some of these characteristics sound similar to that of God in monotheistic Western religions. Finally, in chapter 25 of the Lotus Sutra (one of the most powerful and influential of all the Mahayana sutras), consider the description of the bodhisattva whose name is "Perceiver of the World's Sounds" (another name for Avalokitesvara):

"At that time the Bodhisattva Inexhaustible Intent immediately rose from his seat, bared his right shoulder, pressed his palms together and, facing the Buddha, spoke these words: 'World Honored One, this Bodhisattva Perceiver of the World's Sounds -- why is he called Perceiver of the World's Sounds?'
The Buddha said to Bodhisattva Inexhaustible Intent: 'Good man, suppose there are immeasurable hundreds, thousands, ten thousands, millions of living beings who are undergoing various trials and suffering. If they hear of this Bodhisattva Perceiver of the World's Sounds and single-mindedly call his name, then at once he will perceive the sound of their voices and they will all gain deliverance from their trials.'

'If someone, holding fast to the name of Bodhisattva Perceiver of the World's Sounds, should enter a great fire, the fire could not burn him. This would come about because of this bodhisattva's authority and supernatural power. If one were washed away by a great flood and call upon his name, one would immediately find himself in a shallow place.'

'Suppose there were a hundred, a thousand, ten thousand, a million living beings who, seeking for gold, silver, lapis lazuli, seashell, agate, coral, amber, pearls, and other treasures, set out on the great sea, and supposedly a fierce wind should blow their ship off course and it drifted to the land of rakshasas demons. If among those people there is even just one who calls the name of Bodhisattva Perceiver of the World's Sounds, then all those people will be delivered from their troubles with the rakshasas. This is why he is called Perceiver of the World's Sounds.'" (Watson translation, 1993)

Thus, since there is such a wide range of beliefs and practices in Buddhism across the various traditions, there may be some beliefs at least among the Buddhist laity in different parts of the world that include belief in a divine being that is deeply compassionate, responsive to human needs, and is worshiped as a god or like God.

The Buddha as God

Do some Buddhists pray to and worship the Buddha as Western monotheists worship God? In other words, do Buddhists in some part of the world simply call God by the name Buddha and worship him accordingly? Most traditional Buddhist scholars say that Buddhists do not pray to or worship the Buddha as God, but rather say that such activities -- including the placing of palms together with fingers directed heavenward -- are only gestures of respect and admiration for the Buddha. However, let us examine how the Buddha's own immediate followers considered him after his death. Shortly after the Buddha's death, some of his followers began to build relics of the Buddha to worship and pray to, and it became customary to make pilgrimages to places where he had walked (Religion Facts, 2004).

While there is no saying (sutta) of the Buddha that instructs his followers to love or seek help from him as a divine being, he does advise them to take refuge in the Triple Gem (Dhammayut Order, 2013). As noted earlier, the Triple Gem are the Buddha, the Dhamma, and the Sangha. In fact, the way for someone to convert to Buddhism often involves saying, "I take refuge in the Buddha. I take refuge in the Dhamma. I take refuge in the Sangha." The Dhammapada says:

"But who to the Buddha, Dhamma, and Sangha as refuge has
gone, sees with full insight the Four Noble Truths;
Misery, the arising of misery, and the transcending of misery, the
Noble Eightfold Path leading to the allaying of misery.
This, indeed, is a refuge secure. This is the highest refuge.
Having come to this refuge, one is released from all misery."
(190-192)

Buddhist scholars do not say that taking refuge in the Buddha means
to worship him as a god or God. However, what about lay Buddhists
as they struggle with daily life? Might some misunderstand and
interpret this to mean that they could or should worship and pray to
the Buddha as the Supreme God/Brahman? Do not many Asian
Buddhists have statues of the Buddha in their household shrines or
attend temples with large pictures or statues of the Buddha? Note
this commentary on the Mahayana Lotus Sutra:

"In Mahayana belief, the Buddha has become an all-knowing
being, somewhere between a divine person - a mortal man who
achieves immortality - and a god, to whom even Hindu gods
offer respect. His wisdom surpasses that of the other gods,
because he recognizes the uncreated and infinite nature of the
universe, whereas some of them imagine themselves as
creators." (Anonymous, n.d.)

Williams et al (2012, p 26) also note that later Buddhist tradition held
that the Buddha was *omniscient* (all-knowing), a characteristic that is
usually attributed only to God in Western traditions.

Furthermore, Buddhists are instructed to take refuge in the
Dhamma (the teachings of the Buddha). The Dhamma is described
by Theravada scholar Gethin (1998) as "the basis of things, the
underlying nature of things, the way things are; in short, it is the truth
about things, the truth about the world" (p 35). Might the Dhamma
also be understood as a type of theistic force or concept? Gethin
(1998, p. 30) notes that there is conceptual overlap in the nature of
the Buddha, Dharma, and Brahma in Eastern thought:

"One early Buddhist text puts it that the Buddha is 'one whose body is Dharma, whose body is Brahma; who has become Dharma, who has become Brahma'. Now *dharma* and *brahma* are two technical terms pregnant with emotional and religious meaning. Among other things Dharma is 'the right way to behave', 'the perfect way to act'; hence it is also the teaching of the Buddha since by following the teaching of the Buddha one follows the path that ends in Dharma or perfect action. We have already come across the term Brahma denoting a divine being (p. 24), but in Buddhist texts *brahma* is also used to denote or describe the qualities of such divine beings; thus *brahma* conveys something of the sense of the English 'divine', something of the sense of 'holy' and something of the sense of 'perfection'. Like the English word 'body' the Sanskrit/Pali word *kiiya* means both a physical body and figuratively a collection or aggregate of something-as in 'a body of opinion'. To say that the Buddha is *dharma-kiiya m*eans that he is at once the embodiment of Dharma and the collection or sum of all those qualities -- non-attachment, loving kindness, wisdom, etc. -- that constitute Dharma."

Love, at least non-attached love, is certainly one of the core features of Dhamma, which in its essence involves doing no harm to anyone and instead treating others with compassion (based on the Eightfold Path). The concept of unconditional love (agape) in Christianity is quite similar to this Buddhist view of compassion. The New Testament also describes God in terms of love: "Whoever does not love does not know God, because *God is love*" (1 John 4:8). Thus, in some ways of thinking, the distinction between the terms Buddha, Dhamma, and God becomes somewhat nebulous, and the possibility of overlap between them does exist.

A discussion of the possibility that -- at least from a Western viewpoint -- the Buddha may in some way have been considered divine is the following (Gethin (1998, pp 28-29):

"So what does this transcendence imply about the final nature of a buddha? If one is thinking in categories dictated and shaped by the theologies of Judaism, Christianity, and Islam, and also modern Western thought, there is often a strong inclination to suppose that such a question should be answered in terms of the categories of human and divine: *either* the Buddha was basically a man *or* he was some kind of god, perhaps even God. But something of an imaginative leap is required here, for these are not the categories of Indian or Buddhist thought. In the first place, according to the Buddhist view of things, the nature of beings is not eternally or absolutely fixed. Beings that were once humans or animals may be reborn as gods; beings that were once gods may be reborn as animals or in hellish realms. Certainly, for the Buddhist tradition, the being who became *buddha* or awakened had been born a man, but equally that being is regarded as having spent many previous lives as a god. Yet in becoming a buddha he goes beyond such categories of being as human and divine."

Not clear, however, is what exactly Gethin means by a buddha that is beyond divine. What is beyond divine or beyond Brahman, the Supreme God, which at least in Hinduism means the true essence of everything?[1]

The third of the Three Jewels and object of refuge is the Sangha or Buddhist community of believers who are seeking to follow the Eightfold Path. There is also some resemblance here to the teachings of Jesus, who encouraged followers to love God (here, the Buddha/Dhamma) with all their heart and soul and love their neighbor (Sangha) as their self. The Christian community is sometimes called "the body of Christ." Indeed, others (Borg & Kronfield, 1999) have pointed out the similarities between the sayings of the Buddha and those of Jesus, whom Christians believe is God.

Conclusions

While Buddhism is widely considered a non-theistic religion, I have speculated here about belief in the divine in Buddhism and the Buddha as God, raising the possibility that many Buddhist laypersons (in actual practice) may pray to and worship a divine being or concept that is similar to what Christians, Jews, Muslims, and Hindus pray to and worship, especially when seeking solace and refuge from the agonies of change and loss that characterize life on this earthly plane.

[1] A view of God known as "pantheism" (all is God) or "panentheism" (all is in God)

CHAPTER 4

BUDDHISM TODAY

How does what Buddhists might be taught about Buddhist beliefs, practices, and teachings relate to what Buddhists currently believe and practice, first here in the U.S. and then around the world? Indeed, it is these lay Buddhists (not Buddhist scholars) that mental health professionals are likely to encounter in their clinical practices.

Buddhism in the USA

In the last chapter, I indicated that Buddhism is often described as a non-theistic religion. Is this true for lay Buddhists in the U.S. and around the world? Let's look at systematic surveys of representative, random samples of Buddhist laypersons. In one of the most reputable surveys of Buddhists in the U.S., no fewer than 75% said they believe in God or a universal spirit (Pew Research Center, 2008). With regard to certainty in that belief, among Buddhists who said they believe in God, 39% said they were "absolutely certain" and 28% that they were "fairly certain." Fewer than 1 in 5 (19%) indicated that they did not believe in God.

Other than that, however, there is not much research on the specific beliefs and practices of Buddhists in the U.S. (who make up only 0.7% of the population according to the Pew Research Center, 2008). Nevertheless, there is some evidence in this regard that I will now review. One of the most extensive reports on Buddhists in the

U.S. involved a convenience sample of 1,237 Buddhists (or persons sympathetic to Buddhism) who completed an online survey about their beliefs and practices (Wiist et al., 2010). Given the design of this study and the demographic profile of respondents, it is not clear whether participants were representative of all U.S. Buddhists. Investigators reported that 82% resided in the U.S., 52% lived in the Western US, 50% had graduate or professional degrees beyond completing college, and 90% were white. Thus, this was a highly educated white Caucasian sample that uses the Internet. Even so, however, the findings may provide a glimpse of the religious activities of American Buddhists.

Of those who participated, 72% identified themselves as Buddhist (with the remainder saying they believed in or practiced some aspects of Buddhism); 63% were converts to Buddhism; and 4% were ordained Buddhist monks or nuns. With regard to the branch to which they belonged, 65% practiced only one Buddhist tradition. Of those, 55% practiced Tibetan Buddhism and 22% practiced Zen, Ch'an or Seon Buddhism. More than half (51%) regularly attended meetings of a Buddhist sangha or a Buddhist meditation group; 97% practiced Buddhist meditation, and of those, 61% meditated one or more times per day. Most (81%) of those who meditated had received formal instruction from a monk or nun at a Buddhist temple.

In a subgroup of 886 participants who specifically identified themselves as Buddhists, 99% said they meditated (66% daily or more frequently), 83% chanted or repeated a mantra as part of Buddhist practice, 79% engaged in Buddhist prayer, 47% regularly attended Buddhist gatherings, 16% "very often" attended services at a Buddhist temple, 96% read and studied Buddhist scriptures (38% "very often"), 70% attended a formal retreat or stayed in a monastery, and 76% formally agreed to the "Three Refuges" in the presence of other Buddhists (Wiist et al, 2012). With regard to understanding the Eightfold Path, the following percentages indicated they understood the path and could easily apply it in their daily life or understood it well enough to teach it to others: 57% right understanding, 58% right thought, 63% right speech, 66% right action, 74% right livelihood, 60% right effort, 60% right mindfulness, and 53% right concentration (with the remainder indicating under-standing, but had difficulty applying it in their daily lives). Thus,

Buddhists in the United States appear to be quite religiously active (at least this largely white non-Asian highly educated group that responded to an Internet survey).

Buddhism outside the USA

What about East and Southeast Asia where most of the Buddhists in the world live today? Three large population based surveys of Buddhists in this region of the world have been completed, and the datasets are now downloadable for analysis (**Tables 1-3**) (Koenig, 2016, unpublished report). What do these random national samples of adult Buddhists say about their beliefs and practices?

Belief in God/Buddha. The International Social Survey Program (ISSP, 2008)[1] examined the beliefs of 1,226 Buddhists living in 40 countries around the world, including Taiwan, Japan, and South Korea (primarily Buddhists from the Mahayana branch), comparing them to 45,438 non-Buddhists, and 12,557 persons with no religious affiliation (**Table 1**). A significant proportion of Buddhists (>80%) indicated that they at least sometimes believe in the existence of God or a higher power; only 18.6% said they did not believe in God or didn't know.[2] When asked the question in a different way, i.e., whether they believed in God now or in the past, 69.0% said that they believe in God now (more specifically, 52.1% said they believe in God now and in the past, whereas 16.9% said believe now but not in the past).

---

[1] *International Social Survey Program (2008)* surveyed a random sample of 59,063 citizens ages 15 to 90 from 40 countries (Australia, Austria, Belgium - Flanders, Chile, Croatia, Cyprus, Czech Republic, Denmark, Dominican Republic, Finland, France, Germany, Great Britain, Hungary, Ireland, Israel, Italy, Japan, Latvia, Mexico, Netherlands, New Zealand, Northern Ireland, Norway, Philippines, Poland, Portugal, Russia, Slovakia, Slovenia, Spain, South Korea, South Africa, Sweden, Switzerland, Taiwan, Turkey, Ukraine, Uruguay, the United States of America, Venezuela), including Taiwan, Japan, and South Korea. **Most Buddhists in this sample came from Japan (32.4%), Taiwan (31.9%), and South Korea (29.3%).** Interviews were conducted face-to-face, by telephone, and through self-completed postal questionnaires. The data were downloaded from the Association of Religion Data Archives, www.TheARDA.com, and were collected by Dr. Max Haller and his team at the Institut für Soziologie, Universität Graz, Austria (accessed 11/7/16).

[2] This is perhaps not too surprising given that "dharma" or "laws of karma" may be considered by some to be a "higher power" (consistent with my earlier discussion of similarities between the dharma and God)

Table 1. Comparison of religious beliefs/practices between Buddhists, members of other religious groups, and the non-affiliated: *International Social Survey Program 2008*

	Buddhists % (N)/Mean (SD)	Non-Buddhists % (N)/Mean (SD)	No Affiliation % (N)/Mean (SD)
Sample size	1,224	45,438	12,557
Confidence in R[@] groups (high)	19.9 (229) ***[1]	38.8 (16,913)	8.1 (939)
Trust too much science, not enough in R (agree)	35.8 (401) ns	32.3 (13,793)	15.9 (1,881)
R causes more conflict than peace (no)	32.2 (364) ***	26.6 (11,481)	11.8 (1,411)
R groups have too little power (agree)	9.2 (105) ***	15.9 (6,497)	8.6 (912)
We must respect all religions (agree)	62.7 (717) ***	83.0 (36,841)	69.7 (8,333)
Accept marry relative of different R (yes)	76.1 (849) ns	76.8 (32,721)	82.6 (9,493)
Current belief about God			
I know God really exists, no doubts	17.6 (214) ***	51.4 (23,088)	8.7 (1,083)
I believe in God, with some doubts	20.8 (252)	19.0 (8,533)	7.5 (928)
Believe in higher power, not personal God	18.9 (229)	10.9 (4,915)	20.0 (2,478)
Sometimes believe in God, sometimes not	24.1 (293)	9.1 (4,065)	9.0 (1,108)
Don't know if God exists & can't find out	10.6 (129)	5.8 (2,613)	19.2 (2,373)
I don't believe in God	8.0 (97)	3.8 (1,700)	35.7 (4,416)
Present and past belief in God			
I believe in God now & always have	52.1 (517) ***	79.1 (31,260)	19.2 (1,970)
I believe in God now, but didn't used to	16.9 (168)	8.3 (3,265)	5.2 (529)
Don't believe in God now, but used to	10.2 (101)	6.4 (2,534)	23.4 (2,395)
Don't believe in God now & never have	20.8 (206)	6.2 (2,534)	52.2 (5,347)
Believes in life after death (yes)	60.8 (660) ***	66.2 (27,216)	31.5 (3,569)
Believes in heaven (yes)	54.9 (586) ***	68.9 (28,295)	21.1 (2,390)
Believes in hell (yes)	52.0 (556) **	54.9 (22,388)	16.6 (1,864)
Believes in religious miracles (yes)	48.4 (510) ***	65.5 (27,191)	21.3 (2,437)
Believes in reincarnation (yes)	61.3 (668) ***	36.1 (14,279)	23.2 (2,603)
Believes in Nirvana (yes)	59.7 (611) ***	20.5 (6,401)	14.2 (1,398)
Believes in power of ancestors (yes)	62.6 (690) ***	33.7 (13,243)	22.1 (2,459)
God concerned over humans personally	47.1 (516) ***	61.4 (26,051)	15.6 (1,785)
Life meaningful only because of God	22.2 (251) ***	39.4 (16,988)	7.0 (830)
Own way to connect with God (no church)	30.3 (326) ***	56.8 (24,289)	35.7 (3,844)
Attend R services when 10 yo (1=never)	3.4 (2.0) ***	5.6 (2.6)	3.4 (2.7)
Attending R services now			
Never	9.6 (117) ***	16.4 (7,328)	73.2 (9,062)
Less than once/yr to several times/yr	61.8 (753)	42.8 (19,122)	24.0 (2,979)
Monthly to 2 or 3 times/month	20.7 (252)	14.9 (6,695)	1.5 (188)
Nearly weekly to several times/week	7.9 (96)	26.0 (11,648)	1.3 (157)
Attend R activities other than R services			
Never	41.8 (506) ns	46.0 (20,654)	80.7 (9,565)
Less than once/yr to several times/yr	46.2 (559)	35.7 (16,034)	17.3 (2,051)
Monthly to 2-3 times/month	8.4 (102)	7.9 (3,535)	1.2 (141)
Nearly weekly to several times/week	3.6 (43)	10.4 (4,672)	0.8 (100)

ns not significant, i.e., $p \geq 0.01$; *$p < 0.01$; **$p < 0.001$; ***$p < 0.0001$ by χ^2 for categorical outcomes, Mantel-Haenszel χ^2, for ordinal, analysis of variance for continuous outcomes ([1] applies to difference between Buddhists and non-Buddhists; [2] differences between all 3 groups provided for demographics; not provided are differences in religious belief/activity between non-affiliated and other groups because all are $p < 0.0001$). [@] R= religion or religious.

Table 1 (continued). Comparison of religious beliefs/practices between Buddhists, members of other religious groups, and the non-affiliated

	Buddhists % (N)/Mean (SD)	Non-Buddhists % (N)/Mean (SD)	No Affiliation % (N)/Mean (SD)
Sample size	1,224	45,438	12,557
Frequency of praying			
Never	15.4 (187) ***	15.4 (6,890)	67.7 (8,457)
Less than once/yr to several times/yr	32.9 (400)	20.7 (9,205)	17.9 (2,207)
Once/month to several times/week	27.1 (332)	34.5 (15,381)	8.0 (1,050)
Once/day to several times/day	24.6 (299)	29.5 (13,155)	6.0 (736)
Has R[@] shrine/altar/icon in home (yes)	64.0 (781) ***	53.8 (24,248)	16.8 (2,098)
Visit R holy place other than church			
Never	37.4 (457) ***	42.5 (19,094)	80.3 (10,023)
Less than once/yr to 1-2 times/yr	35.5 (433)	36.1 (16,207)	16.0 (1,981)
Several times/year to once/month	27.1 (331)	21.4 (9,636)	3.7 (451)
How would you describe yourself?			
Very or extremely religious	22.4 (270) **	20.5 (9,126)	2.4 (295)
Somewhat religious	46.2 (557)	44.6 (19,819)	8.7 (1,050)
Neither religious or non-religious	17.8 (215)	19.2 (8,542)	19.8 (2,397)
Somewhat non-religious	7.9 (95)	8.8 (3,893)	17.3 (2,098)
Very or extremely non-religious	5.8 (70)	7.0 (3,096)	51.8 (6,269)
What are your views concerning religion?			
Very little truth in any religion	9.1 (91) ***	11.0 (4,401)	40.5 (4,012)
Basic truths present in many religions	85.1 (850)	67.3 (26,883)	56.3 (5,584)
There is truth only in one religion	5.8 (58)	21.7 (8,677)	3.3 (323)
Follow R, no interest in spirit/sacred (yes)	56.7 (608) **	41.8 (17,208)	7.0 (785)
R help find inner peace/happiness (agree)	83.5 (976) ᵇˢ	83.7 (35,713)	57.0 (6,509)
R help gain comfort during sorrow (agree)	82.7 (958) ***	87.1 (37,303)	69.9 (7,972)
Positive attitude towards Christians (yes)	23.5 (95) ***	74.4 (16,944)	39.5 (2,463)
Positive attitude towards Muslims (yes)	18.3 (71) ***	36.0 (7,598)	19.7 (1,200)
Positive attitude towards Hindus (yes)	19.0 (74) ***	34.0 (6,784)	26.1 (1,532)
Positive attitude towards Buddhists (yes)	84.7 (350) ***	38.5 (7,752)	38.0 (2,276)
Positive attitude towards Jews (yes)	18.1 (70) ***	36.7 (7,533)	25.0 (1,497)
Positive attitude towards atheists (yes)	27.1 (108) ***	30.1 (6,202)	39.4 (2,408)
Religious affiliations			
Buddhist	100.0 (1,224)	0	0
Christian	0	88.6 (40,277)	0
Jewish, Islam, other religions	0	8.4 (3,807)	0
Hinduism or other Eastern religion	0	3.0 (1,368)	0
No religion	0	0	100.0 (12,559)
Age, years	51.7 (16.9) ***	47.0 (17.4)	44.4 (16.4) ***[2]
Education (at least some college)	17.5 (212) *	14.8 (6660)	21.1 (2,619) ***
Income (1-poor to 10-rich)	4.7 (1.7) ***	5.2 (1.9)	5.3 (1.8) ***
Sex (female)	56.9 (697) ᵇˢ	57.3 (26,026)	46.3 (5,809) ***
Marital status (married, live with spouse)	68.3 (831) ***	55.1 (24,831)	49.0 (5,990) ***

ᵇˢ not significant, i.e., p≥0.01; *p<0.01; **p<0.001; ***p<0.0001 by χ^2 for categorical outcomes, Mantel-Haenszel χ^2, for ordinal, analysis of variance for continuous outcomes ([1]applies to difference between Buddhists and non-Buddhists; [2]differences between all 3 groups provided for demographics; not provided are differences in religious belief/activity between non-affiliated and other groups because all are p<0.0001). [@]R= religion or religious.

In a random national survey of over 7,000 adults living in China (Spiritual Life Study of Chinese Residents) (SLSCR, 2007),[1] detailed information about belief was recorded in this communist, largely non-religious country. The sample included 1,168 Buddhists, 246 non-Buddhists, and 5,482 persons with no religion (**Table 2**). Among this random sample of Buddhists in China, 9.2% say that religion is very important in their lives (vs. 25.1% for non-Buddhists affiliated with other religions, p<0.01). Over three-quarters (75.9%) say that they have religious beliefs (vs. 83.6% of non-Buddhists affiliated with other religious traditions, p<0.01). This self-reported finding is consistent with interviewers' observations that only 8.1% of Buddhist households had a "very religious" atmosphere (although this was not significantly different than non-Buddhist religious households at 14.2%). Only 17.9% of Buddhists said they believe God actually exists (7.9% believe in only one true God, 35.5% in many gods). Of those who believe in God or gods, 86.5% say that God/gods are concerned with the well-being of the world (62.6% in their own personal well-being) and 59.2% say that God/gods are involved in worldly affairs (49.0% in their own personal affairs).

Likewise, 68.3% of all Buddhists say the Buddha actually exists (question asked in **the present**). Furthermore, 21.1% of Buddhists say they worship the Buddha (of those, 24.5% do so regularly). When Buddhists who pray are asked *to whom* they pray to, 68.3% say they pray to Buddha. Admittedly, "worship" and "pray to" may mean different things in Eastern society than in the West, but are they really that different? Among factors that influenced the views of Buddhists who believe in the existence of God and Buddha, the primary influence was that of elders in their family (55.2% for belief in God and 59.1% for belief in the Buddha).

---

[1] *Spiritual Life Study of Chinese Residents (2007)* surveyed a random sample of 7,021 Chinese citizens ages 16 to 75 in 2007. Respondents were selected using a multi-stage method to select metropolitan cities, towns and administrative villages. The final survey was administered in 56 locales throughout China, including 3 municipal cities (Beijing, Shanghai, Chongqing), 6 province capital cities (Guangzhou, Nanjing, Wuhan, Hefei, Xi'an and Chengdu). In addition, 11 regional level cities, 16 small towns, and 20 administrative villages were sampled. Kish method used to select one person per household for face-to-face in-home interviews.
The data were downloaded from the Association of Religion Data Archives, www.TheARDA.com, and were collected by Dr. Anna Sun and her research team and was funded by the John Templeton Foundation (accessed 11/7/16).

The third dataset that I examined was the World Values Survey (WVS, 2005-2006),[1] which assessed a random sample of 60,579 adults from 60 countries (**Table 3**). The sample included 3,266 Buddhists. Of those, 1,480 were from Thailand where the majority of the population is from the Theravada branch, and 1,099 were from countries where Buddhists of the Mahayana branch predominate (including 71 from mainland China, 272 from Taiwan, and 160 from Hong Kong). Buddhists in the WVS were more likely than Chinese Buddhists in the SLSCR to say that religion is very important in their lives, although they were considerably less likely than non-Buddhist religions to claim this (38.0% vs. 58.0%, respectively, p<0.0001). Interestingly, Theravada Buddhists were more likely to report that religion is very important to their lives than Mahayana Buddhists by quite a margin (55.6% vs. 13.9%, p<0.0001). Interestingly, this contrasts with the proportion of Theravada Buddhists who view themselves as "religious persons" compared to Mahayana Buddhists (34.3% vs. 52.5%, p<0.0001), which is difficult to understand.

Only one question was inquired about belief in God. The question asked: "How important is God in your life? Please use this scale to indicate: 10 means 'very important' and 1 means 'not at all important.'" Among Buddhists overall, the average rating was 7.0, which while surprisingly high was not quite as high as the rating from members of non-Buddhist religions (8.5, p<0.0001).

---

[1] *World Values Survey 2005-2006* surveyed a random national sample of 83,879 adults ages 18 to 85 from more than 80 countries (approximately 1000 per country using full probability sampling). **Of the 80 countries, one country has Buddhists primarily from the Theravada branch of Buddhism (Thailand [n=1,480]) and the remaining Southeast Asian countries have Buddhists primarily from the Mahayana branch (China [n=71], Japan [n=341], S Korea [n=300], Taiwan [n=227], Hong Kong [n=160]).** The mode of data collection for WVS survey was face-to-face interviewing. This project was carried out by an international network of social scientists, with local funding for each survey. The data were downloaded from the World Values Survey (WORLD VALUES SURVEY Wave 5 2005-2008 OFFICIAL AGGREGATE v.20140429. World Values Survey Association [www.worldvaluessurvey.org]. Aggregate File Producer: Asep/JDS, Madrid SPAIN) retrieved from http://www.worldvaluessurvey.org/WVSDocumentationWV5.jsp (accessed 11-7-16)

Table 2. Comparison of religious beliefs/practices of Buddhists, members of other religious groups, and the non-affiliated: *Spiritual Life Study of Chinese Residents 2007*

	Buddhists % (N)/Mean (SD)	Non-Buddhists % (N)/Mean (SD)	No Affiliation % (N)/Mean (SD)
Sample size	1168	246	5,482
Importance of religion (R)[@]			
Very important	9.2 (102) *[1]	25.1 (60)	0.6 (31)
Somewhat important/unimportant	65.2 (726)	50.6 (121)	24.2 (1,231)
Not at all important	25.7 (286)	24.3 (58)	75.2 (3,823)
Do you have any religious belief? (yes)	75.9 (874) *	83.6 (204)	0.5 (25)
Belief about God? (in non-affiliated) (yes)			
No such thing as God, spirits, Buddha (B)[@]	---	---	77.3 (4,200)
Don't know or hard to say	---	---	10.4 (562)
No religion, but think God, spirits, B exist	---	---	12.3 (669)
Belief about God at age 15			
No such thing as God, spirits or B	42.1 (288) [ns]	52.6 (81)	74.7 (3,978)
Don't know or hard to say	24.1 (165)	16.2 (25)	12.5 (664)
No religion, but think God, spirits, B exist	33.8 (231)	31.2 (48)	12.8 (681)
Attend church/B service in past yr (yes)	1.8 (21) ***	31.8 (77)	0.4 (19)
Worship God/gods in B temp past yr (yes)	63.0 (728) ***	49.4 (118)	7.5 (406)
Worship in B temple in past yr (regular)	16.9 (122) ***	46.2 (54)	5.0 (20)
Worship God/gods at grave/ancest temple	25.8 (298) [ns]	21.8 (52)	44.9 (2,429)
Worship God/gods at home past yr (yes)	4.8 (55) [ns]	5.9 (14)	1.2 (64)
Venerate ancestral spirits by grave past	77.5 (904) ***	38.8 (94)	67.1 (3,640)
Pray, worship, burn incense B temp (yes)	11.0 (128) ***	0.4 (1)	1.1 (58)
Frequency of R activity			
Only on religious or traditional holidays	56.7 (611) ***	28.6 (56)	81.9 (3,033)
Only occasionally	34.4 (371)	32.1 (63)	17.8 (658)
Once or twice a month	7.7 (83)	10.2 (20)	0.3 (12)
Once a week	0.7 (7)	25.0 (49)	0.0 (0)
Daily	0.6 (6)	4.1 (8)	0.1 (2)
Statue or portrait of B in home? (yes)	29.0 (337) ***	2.5 (6)	4.0 (215)
Wore objects/accessories past year?			
Wore B objects in past year (yes)	25.0 (287) ***	1.7 (4)	3.2 (172)
Wore non-B objects or talisman (yes)	8.5 (98)	29.2 (71)	4.4 (236)
Invited to officiate or participate in funeral?			
Invited B monk (yes)	9.0 (83) *	1.2 (2)	2.5 (105)
Invited R leader, Feng-sh	27.8 (257)	28.7 (50)	14.3 (595)
None	63.2 (583)	70.1 (122)	83.2 (3,467)
B activities in past year			
Meditated	2.7 (31) ***	0.8 (2)	0.1 (3)
Recited B prayers	5.9 (69) **	0.4 (1)	0.1 (4)
Worshiped B	21.1 (246) ***	0.8 (2)	1.4 (74)
Read B texts	1.8 (21) [ns]	0.0 (0)	0.0 (1)
Burned incense	9.5 (110) *	3.7 (9)	1.8 (95)
Vegetarian for B reasons	0.9 (11) [ns]	0.8 (2)	0.2 (11)
Other religious activities (non-B)	38.6 (450) ***	66.0 (161)	26.7 (1,457)
None	19.6 (228)*	27.5 (67)	69.8 (3,809)

Table 2 (continued). Comparison of religious beliefs/practices of Buddhists, members of other religious groups, and the non-affiliated

	Buddhists % (N)/Mean (SD)	Non-Buddhists % (N)/Mean (SD)	No Affiliation % (N)/Mean (SD)
Sample size	1168	246	5,482
If yes to Buddhist activities (*previous page*)			
Frequency of meditation (regularly) (reg)	38.7 (12) [ns]	100.0 (2)	0.0 (0)
Frequency of reciting B prayers (reg)	39.3 (35) [ns]	0.0 (0)	25.0 (1)
Frequency of worshiping the B (reg)	24.5 (75) [ns]	0.0 (0)	7.9 (6)
Frequency of read B texts (reg)	44.9 (31) [ns]	0.0 (0)	0.0 (0)
Frequency of burn incense (reg)	26.1 (127) [ns]	19.1 (4)	8.6 (25)
B and non-B superstitious acts			
Hang statue of B in car (last year)	0.9 (10) ***	0.4 (1)	0.5 (27)
Worn red belt/clothes, other superstitious	47.6 (541)	30.0 (73)	25.9 (1,402)
No superstitious acts	51.5 (586)	69.6 (169)	73.6 (3,984)
Ever practiced Qi Gong? (yes)	2.4 (28) [ns]	2.0 (5)	1.0 (56)
If yes, frequency of Qi Gong (no longer)	50.0 (13) [ns]	50.0 (2)	63.3 (31)
Ever pray, communicate with God or supernatural	37.6 (427) ***	56.4 (137)	4.3 (231)
If pray, how often do you pray?			
Less than once or twice/year	64.2 (267) ***	39.4 (52)	70.6 (161)
Several times/week or daily	10.8 (45)	33.3 (44)	4.0 (9)
If pray, to whom do you pray?			
Buddha	68.3 (289) ***	2.2 (3)	38.6 (76)
God	6.6 (28)	16.2 (22)	11.7 (23)
Others	25.1 (106)	81.6 (111)	49.8 (98)
Donated money/goods to R organization	59.1 (679) ***	40.1 (97)	12.7 (692)
Do you think God actually exists? (yes)	17.9 (182) ***	48.9 (111)	4.4 (223)
If yes, who most influenced view?(top 3)			
Elders in family	55.2 (95) **	43.6 (48)	54.9 (112)
Friends	7.0 (12)	4.6 (5)	4.9 (10)
My own reading of books	12.8 (22)	4.6 (5)	9.8 (20)
Do you think god of heaven actual exits?	27.3 (279) **	15.6 (35)	7.2 (364)
If yes, who most influenced view?			
Elders in family	59.3 (156) *	61.8 (21)	61.1 (201)
My own reading of books	8.4 (22)	5.9 (2)	4.6 (15)
R places of worship, church/temple	8.0 (21)	26.5 (9)	0.9 (3)
Do you think evil forces/demons exists?	7.1 (74) [ns]	8.1 (18)	0.8 (43)
If yes, who most influenced this belief?			
Elders in family	45.7 (32) [ns]	33.3 (6)	51.3 (20)
Neighbors	12.9 (9)	11.1 (2)	12.8 (5)
My own reading of books	10.0 (7)	0.0 (0)	0.0 (0)
Do you think heaven actually exists?	17.5 (181) ***	38.4 (86)	3.0 (155)
If yes, who most influenced this belief?			
Elders in family	46.9 (82) **	40.0 (34)	50.0 (73)
My own reading of books	8.0 (14)	2.4 (2)	12.3 (18)
R places of worship, church/temple	13.7 (24)	36.5 (31)	1.4 (2)

Table 2 (continued). Comparison of religious beliefs/practices of Buddhists, members of other religious groups, and the non-affiliated

	Buddhists % (N)/Mean (SD)	Non-Buddhists % (N)/Mean (SD)	No Affiliation % (N)/Mean (SD)
Sample size	1168	246	5,482
Do you think hell/underworld exists?	23.1 (239) ns	27.7 (62)	3.8 (194)
If yes, who most influenced this belief?			
Elders in family	53.5 (123) *	39.3 (24)	55.1 (102)
My own reading of books	6.5 (15)	1.6 (1)	8.1 (15)
R places of worship, church/temple	16.5 (38)	39.3 (24)	1.6 (3)
Do you think Jesus Christ actually exists?	8.3 (84) ***	64.0 (151)	2.1 (105)
If yes, who most influenced this belief?			
Elders in family	43.8 (35) *	34.3 (1)	35.6 (36)
Neighbors	11.3 (9)	6.2 (9)	14.9 (15)
My own reading of books	13.8 (11)	4.8 (7)	13.9 (14)
Do you think a soul actually exits? (yes)	30.2 (318) ns	35.5 (78)	6.2 (311)
If yes, who most influenced this belief?			
Elders in family	56.7 (170) ***	38.2 (29)	52.6 (151)
Other relatives	7.7 (23)	1.3 (1)	7.7 (22)
R places of worship, church/temple	11.3 (34)	39.5 (30)	1.4 (4)
Do you think Buddha actually exists?	68.3 (751) ***	11.5 (25)	6.9 (347)
If yes, who most influenced this belief?			
Elders in family	59.1 (430) ns	48.0 (12)	54.7 (179)
My own reading of books	5.1 (37)	8.0 (2)	8.0 (26)
R places of worship, church/temple	17.6 (128)	28.0 (7)	6.1 (20)
Do you think Karma actually exists? (yes)	47.4 (499) ***	32.7 (71)	17.7 (883)
If yes, who most influenced this belief?			
Elders in family	44.1 (207) ns	40.6 (28)	48.9 (391)
My own reading of books	9.4 (44)	10.1 (7)	13.0 (104)
R places of worship, church/temple	14.1 (66)	17.4 (12)	1.3 (10)
Do you think afterlife actually exists?	23.7 (241) *	13.8 (30)	3.0 (151)
If yes, who most influenced this belief?			
Elders in family	40.4 (92) ns	43.3 (13)	44.4 (60)
My own reading of books	9.7 (22)	13.3 (4)	14.1 (19)
R places of worship, church/temple	21.5 (49)	23.3 (7)	1.5 (2)
Do you think reincarnation actual exists?	20.8 (211) ***	8.3 (18)	2.3 (114)
If yes, who most influenced this belief?			
Elders in family	38.5 (77) ns	41.2 (7)	41.7 (45)
My own reading of books	12.5 (25)	5.9 (1)	16.7 (18)
R places of worship, church/temple	23.0 (46)	29.4 (5)	0.9 (1)
Do you think gods/spirits actual exist?	21.6 (222) ***	8.6 (19)	2.4 (121)
If yes, who most influenced this belief?			
Elders in family	45.8 (97) ns	31.6 (6)	50.9 (58)
My own reading of books	10.9 (23)	5.3 (1)	8.8 (10)
R places of worship, church/temple	16.5 (35)	31.6 (6)	2.6 (3)
Do you think ghosts actually exist? (yes)	20.4 (213) *	12.1 (27)	2.6 (134)
If yes, who most influenced this belief?			
Elders in family	46.1 (94) ns	37.0 (10)	56.4 (71)
My own reading of books	10.3 (21)	3.7 (1)	7.1 (9)
R places of worship, church/temple	12.3 (25)	22.2 (6)	0.8 (1)

Table 2 (continued). Comparison of religious beliefs/practices of Buddhists, members of other religious groups, and the non-affiliated

	Buddhists % (N)/Mean (SD)	Non-Buddhists % (N)/Mean (SD)	No Affiliation % (N)/Mean (SD)
Sample size	1168	246	5,482
Do you think fate/fortune actually exists?	50.7 (538) ***	32.9 (72)	22.3 (1,121)
If yes, who most influenced this belief?			
Elders in family	46.9 (233) ns	43.7 (31)	54.5 (530)
My own reading of books	13.5 (67)	7.0 (5)	10.9 (106)
R places of worship, church/temple	10.7 (53)	19.7 (14)	0.4 (4)
Do you think ancestral spirits exist?	47.8 (505) ***	14.6 (32)	10.9 (551)
If yes, who most influenced this belief?			
Elders in family	71.1 (350) ns	56.3 (18)	77.2 (403)
My own reading of books	4.1 (20)	3.1 (1)	3.6 (19)
R places of worship, church/temple	11.2 (55)	18.8 (6)	1.7 (9)
Karma exists in personal relationships?	68.0 (728) ***	46.2 (103)	42.9 (2,147)
If yes, who most influenced this belief?			
Elders in family	40.7 (277) ns	30.6 (30)	33.9 648)
Spouse or girl/boyfriend	13.5 (92)	13.3 (13)	24.8 (474)
My own reading of books	11.8 (80)	12.2 (12)	10.3 (196)
What is your view of God/gods?			
Only one true God	7.9 (84) ***	53.0 (123)	1.3 (68)
There are many gods	35.5 (377)	7.8 (18)	2.4 (122)
There is no God or gods	24.6 (261)	21.1 (49)	71.8 (3,670)
As humans, cannot know if there is God	32.1 (341)	18.1 (42)	24.5 (1,249)
If believe in God or gods (n=849).			
God or gods concerned with well-being			
of the world (agree)	86.5 (371) ns	85.1 (114)	60.2 (103)
God/gods concerned with my well-being	62.6 (256) ns	69.3 (88)	38.9 (65)
God/gods involved in worldly affairs	59.2 (236) ns	68.3 (64)	35.2 (58)
God/gods directly involved in my affairs	49.0 (191) ns	61.3 (76)	23.2 (39)
God/gods will answer all prayers	54.2 (211) ns	57.6 (72)	21.9 (35)
Do you think soul exists after death?	35.2 (405) **	46.9 (115)	7.2 (388)
If not no (n=2294), where do you think soul goes?			
The underworld	11.7 (85) ***	5.4 (9)	9.9 (138)
Heaven or hell	24.3 (177)	62.9 (105)	12.7 (177)
Soul will wander in human world	7.4 (54)	1.8 (3)	4.0 (56)
Become spirits or Buddha	5.9 (43)	0.6 (1)	0.6 (9)
Reincarnation	18.4 (134)	6.6 (11)	9.2 (129)
Main influence on your personal actions			
& moral outlook (answer: religion)	2.9 (33) ***	14.9 (36)	0.4 (22)
Observer-rated			
Reliability of answers (not at all)	2.3 (27) ns	2.4 (6)	2.9 (160)
R atmosphere of household			
Very religious	8.1 (95) ns	14.2 (35)	1.2 (67)
Somewhat religious	58.5 (683)	52.4 (129)	16.1 (883)
Not at all	33.4 (390)	3.3 (82)	82.7 (4,532)

Table 2 (continued). Comparison of religious beliefs/practices of Buddhists, members of other religious groups, and the non-affiliated

Demographics	Buddhists % (N)/Mean (SD)	Non-Buddhists % (N)/Mean (SD)	No Affiliation % (N)/Mean (SD)
R affiliations			
Buddhist	100.0 (1,168)	0	0
Daoism	0	9.8 (24)	0
Confucianism	0	4.9 (12)	0
Protestantism	0	67.1 (165)	0
Catholicism	0	6.1 (15)	0
Islam	0	12.2 (30)	0
Don't belief in anything/no R belief	0	0	100.0 (5,482)
Age	40.3 (13.8) [ns]	38.9 (12.7)	39.9 (13.6) [ns 2]
Education level (at least some college)	15.7 (183) [ns]	19.9 (49)	19.2 (1,055) [ns]
Income (city residents) (1-18, low to high)	3.4 (2.6) [ns]	3.3 (2.0)	3.3 (2.1) [ns]
Income (rural residents) (1-18, low to high)	11.4 (5.7) [ns]	10.9 (5.5)	10.4 (5.7) [ns]
Area type (city vs. town and country)	46.7 (545) [ns]	50.8 (125)	40.4 (2,710) [ns]
Gender (female)	59.1 (690) [ns]	65.0 (160)	49.8 (2,728) ***
Marital status (married)	78.4 (913) [ns]	78.4 (192)	78.7 (4,299) [ns]

[ns] not significant, i.e., $p \geq 0.01$; *$p<0.01$; **$p<0.001$; ***$p<0.0001$ by χ^2 for categorical outcomes, Mantel-Haenszel χ^2, for ordinal, and analysis of variance for continuous outcomes ([1]applies to difference between Buddhists and non-Buddhists; [2]differences between all 3 groups provided for demographics; not provided are differences in religious belief/activity between non-affiliated and other groups because all are $p<0.0001$). [@]R=religious or religion, B=Buddha or Buddhist

Interestingly, Theravada Buddhists were more likely to report that religion is very important to their lives than Mahayana Buddhists by quite a margin (55.6% vs. 13.9%, p<0.0001). Interestingly, this contrasts with the proportion of Theravada Buddhists who view themselves as "religious persons" compared to Mahayana Buddhists (34.3% vs. 52.5%, p<0.0001), which is difficult to understand. It would be interesting to know what "religious person" meant to those who answered these questions or how this was translated into the different languages. It would also be interesting to know how the different cultures use standards for answering such a question. Research has shown that people who are more qualified at a task rate themselves as less competent than those who are actually less qualified. Perhaps something similar is happening here, although this is pure speculation.

Only one question was inquired about belief in God. The question asked: "How important is God in your life? Please use this scale to indicate: 10 means 'very important' and 1 means 'not at all important.'" Among Buddhists overall, the average rating was 7.0, which while surprisingly high was not quite as high as the rating from members of non-Buddhist religions (8.5, p<0.0001). Again, Theravada Buddhists scored higher than Mahayana Buddhists (8.0 vs. 5.9, p<0.0001); this is despite the claim by Buddhist scholars that Theravada Buddhism is less theistic than Mahayana Buddhism. In addition, Theravada Buddhists scored higher on all other measures of religious activity. With regard to Mahayana Buddhism, it is important for future research to survey Buddhists in countries or ethnic groups that are dominant Buddhist, such as Bhutan, Tibet (ethnic group), perhaps Mongolia, etc. In conclusion, the findings above support the claim that many Buddhists believe in and worship God, and that at least some Buddhists may view and treat Buddha as non-Buddhists view and treat God (if we assume that those who answered this survey understand the term "God" as westerners do).

Other Buddhist beliefs. The classical core teachings of Buddhism do not include belief in life after death, heaven or hell, the supernatural power of ancestors, demons or evil forces, god of heaven (or other gods and spirits), the soul, religious miracles, or a God that has concern over humans personally.[1] Core Buddhist

---

[1] Bear in mind, though, that (a) reincarnation is a kind of life after death, (b) there is the "hell realm" in Buddhist cosmology, and (c) traditional stories about the

beliefs do include belief in karma, reincarnation, and Nirvana.

In the 2008 ISSP (**Table 1**), 60.8% of Buddhists said they believed in life after death, 54.9% in heaven, 52.0% in hell, 48.4% in religious miracles, 62.6% in the supernatural power of ancestors, and 47.1% said they believed that *God is concerned over humans personally*. Surprisingly, about the same percentages said they believed in reincarnation (61.3%) and Nirvana (59.7%); non-traditional and traditional Buddhist beliefs, then, appear nearly equally as common.

In the 2007 SLSCR (**Table 2**), a smaller percentage of Chinese Buddhists (who were generally less religious than Buddhists in other areas of the world) indicated they believed in the existence of an afterlife (23.7%), a soul (30.2%), heaven (17.5%), hell/underworld (23.1%), god of heaven (27.3%), other gods and spirits (21.6%), ghosts (20.4%), and evil forces/demons (7.1%). More common was belief in ancestral spirits (47.8%) and fate or fortune (50.7%). Among core Buddhist beliefs, belief in reincarnation was low (20.8%) as was belief that the soul is reincarnated after death (27.2%). More common was belief in karma (47.4%), especially karma in personal relationships (68.0%). Such beliefs were primarily influenced by family elders, by participants' own reading, and by places of worship.

Buddhist practices. The 2008 ISSP reported that 7.9% of Buddhists attended religious services weekly or several times per week, significantly less frequent than for religiously affiliated non-Buddhists (26.0%, p<0.0001) (**Table 1**). Frequency of religious activities other than attending religious services was not significantly different between Buddhists and members of non-Buddhist religions (3.6% vs. 10.4% weekly or more than weekly), although frequency of visiting religious holy places other than the church/temple was somewhat more frequent in Buddhists than among non-Buddhists (62.6% vs. 57.5%, p<0.0001). Buddhists were also more likely to have a religious shrine, altar, or icon in their homes (64.0% vs. 53.8% of non-Buddhist religions, p<0.0001). Prayer was similar between Buddhists and non-Buddhists, at least among those who prayed at least once per day (24.6% vs. 29.5%).

Buddha do involve the supernatural power of ancestors, demons or evil forces, gods and spirits, and religious miracles.

Table 3. Comparison of religious beliefs/practices and demographics between Buddhists, members of non-Buddhist groups, and the non-affiliated: *World Values Survey 2005-2006*

	Buddhists % (N)/Mean (SD)	Non-Buddhists % (N)/Mean (SD)	No Affiliation % (N)/Mean (SD)
Sample size	3,266	64,737	14,631
Importance of religion (R)[@]			
Very important	38.0 (1219) ***[1]	58.0 (36,457)	7.2 (963)
Rather important	37.4 (1198)	23.5 (14,756)	14.1 (1886)
Not very important	19.5 (626)	13.3 (8378)	35.8 (4807)
Not at all important	5.1 (163)	5.1 (3224)	43.0 (5770)
Importance of R by Buddhist Branch			
Theravada (n=1,480) (very important)	55.6 (821) ***[2]		
Mahayana (n=1,099) (very important)	13.9 (146)		
Should instill R qualities in child (yes)	21.6 (706) ***	49.1 (32,445)	6.9 (1013)
Should instill R qualities by B branch			
Theravada	28.6 (424) ***		
Mahayana	9.3 (102)		
Active member of religious organization	16.5 (508) ***	24.5 (15,118)	2.2 (290)
Active member by B branch			
Theravada	19.0 (280) ***		
Mahayana	11.0 (101)		
Frequency of R attendance (>/=once/wk)	28.2 (916) ***	42.0 (26,758)	2.4 (284)
Frequency of R attendance by B branch			
Theravada	41.6 (617) ***		
Mahayana	6.2 (67)		
Self-identify as R person			
Religious person	48.2 (1556) ***	81.4 (52,030)	21.8 (3025)
Not a religious person	48.7 (1573)	17.0 (10,863)	57.1 (7949)
A convinced atheist	3.0 (98)	1.5 (961)	21.1 (2937)
Self-identify as R person by B branch			
Theravada (religious)	34.3 (509) ***		
Mahayana (religious)	52.5 (565)		
Theravada (not religious)	65.5 (972)		
Mahayana (not religious)	44.4 (478)		
Theravada (atheist)	0.2 (3)		
Mahayana (atheist)	3.1 (33)		
Importance of God in life			
(1-10 scale, low to hi)	7.0 (2.4) ***	8.5 (2.4)	4.3 (3.3)
Importance of God in life by B branch			
Theravada	8.0 (1.4) ***		
Mahayana	5.9 (2.5)		
Have moments of prayer or meditation?	67.4 (2000) ***	83.2 (47,401)	41.3 (3960)
Moments of prayer/meditate by B branch			
Theravada	75.8 (1118) ***		
Mahayana	57.9 (489)		

Table 3 (continued). Comparison of religious beliefs/practices and demographics between Buddhists, members of non-Buddhist groups, and the non-affiliated

	Buddhists % (N)/Mean (SD)	Non-Buddhists % (N)/Mean (SD)	No Affiliation % (N)/Mean (SD)
Demographics			
R affiliations			
Protestant	0	18.0 (11,653)	0
Catholic	0	29.2 (18,889)	0
Orthodox	0	14.2 (9,193)	0
Jewish	0	0.2 (49)	0
Islam	0	23.1 (13,962)	0
Hindu	0	3.0 (1,962)	0
Buddhist	100.0 (3,266)	0	0
Other religion	0	12.3 (7,929)	0
None	0	0	100.0 (14,631)
Age, years	45.2 (15.9) ***	41.2 (16.6)	42.0 (15.9) ***[3]
Theravada	45.5 (15.7) ***		
Mahayana	49.3 (15.2)		
Education (% at least some college)	17.8 (579) *	20.0 (13,148)	25.9 (3,771) ***
Theravada	12.3 (181) ***		
Mahayana	26.4 (288)		
Financial status (1-10, poor to rich)	5.2 (2.1) ***	4.5 (2.3)	4.7 (2.4) ***
Theravada	5.6 (1.9) ***		
Mahayana	4.4 (2.2)		
Sex (female)	53.3 (1,739) [ns]	53.2 (35,129)	46.5 (6,793) ***
Theravada	51.3 (759)		
Mahayana	56.1 (616)		
Marital status (married)	67.0 (2,180) ***	55.4 (36,538)	50.8 (7,397) ***
Theravada	69.9 (1,036) [ns]		
Mahayana	72.1 (789)		

[ns] not significant, i.e., $p \geq 0.01$; *$p < 0.01$; **$p < 0.001$; ***$p < 0.0001$ by χ^2 for categorical outcomes, Mantel-Haenszel χ^2, for ordinal, and analysis of variance for continuous outcomes ([1]applies to difference between Buddhists and non-Buddhists; [2]differences between Theravada and Mahayana branches; [3]differences between all 3 groups provided for demographics; not provided are differences in religious belief/activity between non-affiliated and other groups because all are $p < 0.0001$). [@]R= religion or religious

The 2007 SLSCR provides the most detailed information on Buddhist religious practices, although the data are limited to Buddhists in China (**Table 2**). Only 1.8% of Chinese Buddhists *attended religious services* at churches, Buddhist or Daoist temples in the past year, but 63.0% *worshiped God/gods* in conventional religious settings such as churches, Buddhist and/or Daoist temples during the past year (16.9% regularly). A few (4.8%) also worshiped God or gods/spirits at home during the past year. Most, however, venerated ancestral spirits at their graves during the past year (77.5%), which was also common among members of non-Buddhist religions (38.8%) and those with no religious affiliation (67.1%).

With regard to prayer, 11.0% of Chinese Buddhists prayed, worshiped, or burned incense at a Buddhist temple in the past year. Some also recited Buddhist prayers (5.9%) during the past year (and of those, 39.3% regularly). Buddhist meditation was uncommon, with only 2.7% (31 of 1,168 Buddhists) indicating that they engaged in this activity during the past year (of those, only 38.7% did so regularly, n=12). Likewise, only 1.8% (n=21) read Buddhist texts during the past year. Burning incense was a bit more common (9.5% in the past year), although being vegetarian for Buddhist reasons was not (0.9%). Interestingly, one of the most common practices among Chinese Buddhists was engaging in non-Buddhist activities (38.6%), especially venerating ancestors (including deceased family members) or praying/communicating with God or a certain supernatural power, asking for blessings and protection generally. Oher Buddhist religious activities include wearing Buddhist objects in the past year (25.0%), hanging a statue of the Buddha in their car (0.9%), and practicing Qi Gong (2.4% ever, n=28, although less than half currently, n=13). Chinese Buddhists, though, tend to be less religious than Buddhists in other East Asian countries (possibly due to Communist rule during the latter half of the 20th century).

In the 2005-2006 WVS, 16.5% of Buddhists said they were active members of a religious organization, especially those from the Theravada branch (Thailand) (19.0%) (**Table 3**). Even more said they attended religious services once per week or more (28.2%), again Theravada Buddhists in particular (41.6%). Over two-thirds (67.4%) said that they take moments for prayer or meditation (75.8% of Theravada Buddhists), in contrast to that in Chinese Buddhists, where only 2.7% meditated (although "taking moments for prayer or meditation" does not necessarily involve regular practice, and prayer was not distinguished from meditation in that question).

Conclusions

Thus, based on recent surveys of Buddhists from around the world, beliefs and activities appear to have veered considerably from the core Buddhist teachings in original Buddhist texts. The Buddha did not emphasize belief in or worship of God, gods/spirits, ancestors, or himself, nor did he encourage belief in life after death, the soul, heaven, hell, demons/evil forces, religious miracles, or prayer to him or other gods, and yet that is what many Buddhists do today. Except in Thailand, where Theravada Buddhists predominate, Buddhists tend to be less religious than members of other religious faiths in East Asia, especially in China (where nearly half of the world's Buddhists currently reside). Furthermore, belief in reincarnation, Nirvana, and karma (which the Buddha did emphasize) is far from uniform among Buddhists today, especially those in China where only one in five believe in reincarnation (20.8%), less than half believe in karma (47.4%), and few read Buddhist religious texts (1.8%) or meditate (2.7%) (only 1.0% regularly). The beliefs and practices of Buddhists in many areas of the world today, then, are far different than did the original followers of the Buddha. Practices of Buddhists in the United States and other Western countries may also be quite different from Buddhists living in other areas of the world, based on Internet surveys (Wiist et al 2010; 2012). Thus, mental health professionals should not assume that a Buddhist patient believes and practices in the same way that early Buddhists did.

CHAPTER 5

BUDDHISM AND MENTAL HEALTH:

SPECULATIONS

How might the beliefs and practices of Buddhists affect their mental health or influence the treatments that Buddhists seek when they experience mental health problems? In this chapter I speculate on the positive and negative effects of Buddhist beliefs and practices on mental health.

Positive Effects

Buddhism is a religion, but it is more than that. It is a philosophy for living couched in an Eastern worldview. The core teachings in Buddhism directly address the fact that people emotionally suffer and argue that there is a way to relieve that suffering. The Eightfold Path describes the way as perceived by the Buddha, and every step is aimed at initiating, maintaining, or improving mental health. Here are the eight steps in the path and their expected mental health consequences.

(1) <u>Right Understanding</u>. Buddhism claims that suffering is part of the human condition, nothing is permanent, and lasting happiness cannot be achieved through relationships, occupation, or material possessions. This belief is essential to having a right view of the world. Therefore, one might expect that practicing Buddhists would be more able to accept loss and change, rather than have unrealistic expectations of continual happiness and fight against the inevitable disruptions and disappointments associated with living, which often result in depression, anxiety and distress.

(2) <u>Right Intention</u>. Buddhism motivates adherents to renounce attachments and stop clinging to pleasures, people, fame, power, or anything that might lead to greed or disregard for the well-being of others. Thus, Buddhists are encouraged to hold onto things lightly (like gently holding a frightened bird in the palm of the hand, without crushing it). Again, such a view should result in less anger, less anxiety, and less emotional pain when losses occur or expectations are not met.

(3) <u>Right Action</u>. Buddhism prescribes certain behaviors (compassion, kindness towards others) and proscribes others (cheating, stealing, dishonesty, sexual misconduct). Such "prosocial" behaviors (and avoidance of antisocial ones) should promote good social relationships and increase the availability of social supports when needed during times of stress. Right action should also result in a lower likelihood of being put in prison, fired from work, or divorce from a spouse or partner as a result of wrong actions, all reducing stress and vulnerability to mental health problems.

(4) <u>Right Speech</u>. Speaking softly, gently, affectionately, and avoiding lying or gossiping should inevitably lead to better relationships with others, including those with family members and with colleagues at work and during play. Again, this should increase the likelihood of having people around to support and encourage one when needed to combat depression and anxiety.

(5) <u>Right Livelihood</u>. This involves pursuing an occupation that does not involve trickery or cheating others, and instead one that deals fairly and up front with colleagues in business. The Buddhist's

conviction is to avoid anything that might increase the suffering of others. Being content with less, not constantly wanting more, and not being willing to harm others for selfish gains (due to unrestrained greed) should enhance relationships at home and at work, and ultimately reduce stress and promote mental health.

(6) Right Effort. This Buddhist principle emphasizes that through personal effort an individual can make constructive changes in thought and behavior and pursue a life that minimizes their own suffering and that of others. It includes stopping whatever thoughts or behaviors that are preventing right action. This, in fact, is the essential purpose of cognitive behavioral therapy (CBT). Central to the success of CBT is motivation at the cognitive level to alter core beliefs and challenge dysfunctional cognitions, and change behaviors that are self-defeating. If this Buddhist belief increases efforts to think and behave in positive ways, then it should enhance mental health.

(7) Right Mindfulness. Keeping thoughts in the present, being open to whatever arises, and avoiding wandering thoughts of the past or the future are emphasized here. The application of this principle may help to avoid concerns and ruminations about the past and prevent worries about the future that contribute to mental distress. Indeed, mindfulness meditation has today become incorporated into many standard psychotherapeutic approaches (particularly CBT) for the treatment of emotional problems (and many other mental disorders).

(8) Right Concentration. This involves focusing on a single object and excluding everything else in order to quiet the mind and bring it under control, leading to deep states of peace and well-being. Such concentration is likely to move consciousness away from disturbing thoughts to present-centered quietness. Again, the purpose of this pathway (as in every step of the Eightfold Path) is to promote a healthy state of mind and relieve anxiety and distress.

There is every reason, then, to expect that Buddhists who follow these principles should experience greater peace, happiness, and better mental health overall. Almost every emotional disorder, then, should be less prevalent and psychological well-being greater among

Buddhists who follow the Eightfold Path. In fact, these principles should be applicable in the treatment of individuals with mental disorder more generally in Buddhists and non-Buddhists. Such an approach, for example, might be particularly useful for individuals with addictive disorders (a form of pathological "attachment") (see Groves & Farmer, 1994).

Worsening Mental Health

As with other world religions, Buddhism is unlikely to have only positive effects and the potential for negative effects on mental health is also there. For example, the experience of deep meditative states without professional guidance can lead to (or uncover) dissociative (Waelde, 2004) or psychotic symptoms (Kuijpers et al., 2007; Vives et al., 2011), including the precipitation of manic episodes (Yorston, 2001). Thus, practicing various forms of Buddhist meditation – particularly the deeper stages of Jhana (stages 5 through 8) – may have untoward consequences for the novice, particularly if vulnerable to mental illness.

The emphasis in Buddhism on asceticism could promote self-harm (as the Buddha almost experienced at the beginning of his search), and detachment from friends/family may also lead to social isolation, particularly among those who misunderstand the Buddha's teachings. Williams et al (2012, p 2) note that "Buddhism is thus a highly individualistic path of liberation. One is bound by one's own mind, and it is by working on one's own mind that one becomes liberated, attaining the highest possible spiritual goal." With regard to relationships, attachment to others in Buddhism is discouraged (as is attachments of any kind). Again, this may increases the risk of social isolation and withdrawal from the world, especially among those with mental disorders (schizophrenia, social anxiety) or personality traits (anti-social) who take this teaching too far.

Regarding suicide, the Pali Canon is equivocal with regard to the permissibility of ending one's life, where such an action is both "censored and condoned" (Wiltshire 1983; Keown 1996). Addressing this point, De La Vallée Poussin (1922, p. 25) wrote that: "We have therefore good reason to believe (1) that suicide is not an ascetic act leading to spiritual progress and to nirvana, and (2) that no saint or arhat—a spiritually perfect being—will kill himself. But we are confronted with a number of stories which prove beyond dispute that we are mistaken in these two important conclusions."

While every step of the Eightfold Path would hopefully lead to mental health and the relief of suffering, it may not always do so. It is difficult for imperfect humans to think and act in a "right" manner. The self-discipline required may simply be too much for many frail humans whose powerful passions and attachments have come to rule their lives. As indicated in the systematic research above, many Buddhists do not believe or practice in the way that the Buddha intended or that is prescribed in Buddhist texts. Not following the Eightfold Path, Buddhists believe, may result in bad karma and delay their progression towards enlightenment, causing some to feel hopelessness, guilt or shame for their inability to live up to such high standards. This is a challenge that the followers of all the major world religions must struggle with.

Conclusions

Buddhist beliefs and practices arose out of Hinduism over 2500 years ago with the life and teachings of Siddhartha Gautama (the Buddha). After years of struggle and during a deep meditative state, the Buddha arrived at the Four Noble Truths that address the cause of suffering and the way to relieve it through the Eightfold Path. Based on conventional wisdom and simple logic, following the Buddha's teachings and adhering to the Eightfold Path should lead to the relief of suffering and improve mental health. However, many Buddhists in the world today do not strictly follow the Buddha's teachings, but rather integrate Buddhist teachings with those of other religions and local beliefs, traditions, or customs. Many Buddhists may not have read about or studied classic Buddhist texts, and following the Eightfold Path may be difficult for many ordinary people struggling to survive in resource-limited areas of the world (other than those pursuing the life of a monk or a nun). Nevertheless, if followed and adhered to, Buddhist beliefs and practices should result in better mental health and greater well-being. The question that now remains is whether objective systematic research shows that Buddhists experience more peace, happiness and well-being than members of other religions (or no religion), and if greater adherence to Buddhist teachings is associated with greater well-being. The next two chapters will examine that research.

CHAPTER 6

EARLY RESEARCH

This chapter and the next one focus on quantitative research that examines the relationship between Buddhist beliefs/practices and mental health. The purpose is to identify and document the evidence on which to make recommendations for application to clinical practice (Chapter 8). The research will be presented for two periods: early research (1950-2010) and recent research (2010-present). Excluded here are studies of Western forms of mindfulness meditation not firmly grounded within traditional Buddhist beliefs and practices (a literature that has been extensively reviewed elsewhere). While almost all of the research presented here is quantitative, a few qualitative studies have been included to provide a deeper understanding of how Buddhism is related to mental health.

The review of early research in the present chapter is based on studies identified in two editions of the *Handbook of Religion and Health*. The first edition of the *Handbook* provided a systematic review of the world literature on religion and health, and identified 6 studies on religious involvement and mental health in Buddhists published prior to the year 2000 (Koenig et al., 2001). The second edition of the *Handbook* systematically reviewed quantitative research conducted between 2000 and 2010, identifying 16 studies on religion and mental health in Buddhists (Koenig et al., 2012).

Before reviewing that early research, a comment about methodology is necessary. Since almost no measures of Buddhist beliefs and practices existed prior to the year 2000, the amount of research on religiosity and mental health among Buddhists during that period is limited (only 6 studies). When religiosity was assessed among Buddhists during this time, it was typically measured by scales developed for Christian populations. Words in those scales such as church, God, and Bible were modified for a Buddhist population. In 1997 a scale designed specifically for assessing religiosity in Buddhists was published. This was the 11-item Buddhist Beliefs and Practices Scale (Emavardhana and Tori, 1997). Unfortunately, the full instrument has been difficult to obtain, and other than providing a few of the questions on the scale as examples, the full scale was not reported in the article. The psychometric properties of the scale have been reported, although details are few (Tori, 2004, p 41). As a result, not much research has used the scale when examining relationships between religiosity and mental health in Buddhists.

The 26 studies summarized below are categorized into those examining coping with stress, anxiety, depression, and suicide, substance use/abuse, psychological well-being/life satisfaction, quality of life/self-rated health, personality traits, and intervention studies.

Coping with Stress
<u>Torture and abuse</u>. Holtz (1998) compared 35 refugee Tibetan nuns (76%) and lay students (24%) in India who had been arrested and tortured in Tibet because of their religious beliefs, and compared them to 35 Tibetan controls who had not received such treatment. Anxiety symptoms, depressive symptoms, somatic complaints, and social impairments were assessed using the Hopkins Checklist-25. Although anxiety symptoms were higher in those experiencing torture compared to controls (54% vs. 29%), there was no difference in depressive symptoms between the tortured and the controls. Investigators were intrigued by the finding that those experiencing torture did not have more depressive symptoms. They hypothesized

(based on explanations provided by participants) that Tibetan Buddhism helped the 80% of refugee Buddhist nuns by providing an explanation for suffering (due to karma from previous lives) that gave meaning to what they had experienced. By accepting and dealing with their situation in a proper manner and performing good works in this life, they believed that this would provide positive karma that would improve their next lives. Researchers referred to the Buddha's teaching that one's own suffering is little compared to the suffering of others, and in fact, could be utilized to reduce the suffering of others. One of the most sacred spiritual doctrines in Buddhism is that one's own suffering is unimportant and must be transcended. These beliefs, investigators hypothesized, contributed to the psychological resilience seen in the tortured refugees.

In another study of survivors of torture, Keller and colleagues (2006) collected information on a convenience sample of 325 patients attending a Bellevue Hospital/New York University program intended for such victims. Participants included 23% Buddhists, 28% Christians, and 44% Muslims; average age was 34 years and the most heavily represented country was Tibet (22%). Depression, anxiety and PTSD symptoms were assessed using standard measures. Over 80% of patients met criterion levels for significant anxiety, 85% for depression, and 46% for PTSD. Religious affiliation was associated with severity of psychological distress. Buddhists (almost all of whom were from Tibet) experienced fewer PTSD symptoms than Christians ($p < 0.05$) or Muslims ($p < 0.10$). Buddhist affiliation, however, was not associated with depressive or anxiety symptoms. Researchers concluded that "Tibetan Buddhists appear to be less prone to PTSD symptoms than other survivors of torture, despite experiencing comparable traumatic experiences" (p 193).

Sachs and colleagues (2008) interviewed 769 Tibetans residing at the Tibetan Refugee Reception Center in Dharamsala, India, to examine the relationship between types of trauma and anxiety, depressive, somatic, and PTSD symptoms. Most participants (83%) were ages 16-25 years, male (85%), and never married (95%); over half (52%) worked as either a monk or nun in Tibet; 11% reported being tortured; and 75% experienced religious restrictions in Tibet. Coping behaviors were assessed using the Daily Coping Scale (Stone & Neale) made up of eight categories of coping, one of which was religious coping. In addition, three religious Tibetan Buddhist practices/beliefs were enquired about: (1) meditation, (2) seeking divinations from lamas/performing special prayers/visiting temples, and (3) explaining the trauma as due to karma. Among all coping behaviors, religious ones were the most common, with all three Tibetan Buddhist practices/beliefs reported by over 90% of participants, more prevalent than even seeking emotional support from loved ones, friends or professionals (77%). Overall coping activity was associated with *more* depression, anxiety, PTSD, and somatization. Unfortunately, associations between religious coping behaviors (apart from overall coping) and psychological symptoms were not reported.

Caregiver stress. Sethabouppha and Kane (2005) conducted a qualitative study that examined the experiences of 15 Thai Buddhist family caregivers of seriously mentally ill family members. The purpose was to better understand the Buddhist perspective on caregiving. Mentally ill family members being cared for ranged in age from 22 to 50, about half were women, and the majority had less than a grade school education. Five themes were uncovered from the interviews: (1) caregiving is based heavily on Buddhist belief (karma, merit, demerit, past life and rebirth, and dharma); (2) caregiving involves compassion (caring, support); (3) caregiving requires management of emotions (through distraction, religious practice, withdrawal, tolerance, positive thinking, help seeking, and following the Noble Eightfold Path); (4) caregiving requires acceptance (incurable illness, sickness is natural); and (5) caregiving involves suffering (physical burden, emotional distress, economic problems, social problems, knowledge deficit). Researchers concluded that Buddhist beliefs are intimately related to the capacity to care for mentally ill family members.

Medical illness. Tzeng and Yin (2008) surveyed 1,031 medical patients and family visitors at a medical hospital in southern Taiwan (three-quarters of participants were family visitors). Primary religious affiliations of participants were Confucianism, Buddhism, Taoism, Christianity, and Islam (percentage of each group not given). Examined were religious practices used by medical patients or family members to help cope with the medical illness. Religious practices included praying to Buddha (45%) or to other gods of Chinese folklore (24%), and attending a church or temple service to offer prayer (57%) for the medical condition. Approximately one quarter of participants prayed to the gods of two or more religious traditions. The most common religious resources that participants indicated they might need during hospitalization were religious care provided by a physician or nurse (45%), religious services provided by other hospital staff, clergy, or volunteers (28%), and a place to pray such as a prayer room or chapel (19%). Researchers concluded that the majority of patients and family members were involved in prayer or attending religious services as a way of coping with the medical illness.

Tsunami survivors. Hollifield and colleagues (2008) surveyed 89 Sri Lankan adults (average age 45 years) approximately two years after the 2004 Asian tsunami. Assessed were trauma exposure, anxiety, depression, PTSD, and somatic symptoms, along with coping behaviors used to deal with these symptoms. Among participants, 21% were diagnosed with PTSD, 16% scored above the cutoff for significant depression, and 30% scored above the cutoff for significant anxiety. The most common coping behaviors reported by participants as very or extremely helpful were (1) utilizing their own strength (70%), (2) family and friends (56%), and (3) religious practices (53%). *Bodhi-puja* was reported by 44% to be very or extremely helpful. Bodhi-puja involves veneration or worship of the Bodhi tree, which has been a common Buddhist practice in this region since a sapling of the original Bodhi tree (under which the Buddha attained Enlightenment) was brought to Sri Lanka from India in the third century BCE.

Wickrama and Wickrama (2008) analyzed data on 325 mothers of tsunami-affected families in southern Sri Lanka collected 3 to 4 months after the 2004 tsunami. PTSD symptoms and depressive symptoms were assessed. Although religious affiliation of participants was not given, over 70% of the population of Sri Lanka are Theravada Buddhists. Results indicated that 20% had symptoms qualifying them for a diagnosis of PTSD, while 38% scored above the cutoff of 16 on the CESD for significant depressive symptoms. Religious activity was significantly and inversely related to PTSD symptoms (B=-0.16, t=-3.32), but was unrelated to depressive symptoms (B=-0.09, t=-1.80) after controlling for other resilience factors (cohesion and support from family members, number of children, community support, hardiness). Researchers concluded that family support and religious participation were helpful in reducing the detrimental effects of the tsunami on participants' PTSD symptoms. Explaining the effect of religion, they stated: "Buddhists possess relatively more 'awareness' about unavoidable constant change and instability of living and nonliving things and tend to appraise disastrous events and circumstances less negatively because they believe that these events are unavoidable and unalterable life circumstances" (p. 1004).

Levy and colleagues (2009) also interviewed 264 tsunami survivors (90% Buddhist, average age 38, 65% losing close family members, 29% physically injured) six months after the 2004 tsunami devastated Sri Lanka. The purpose of this study was to examine beliefs they had concerning the cause of this disastrous tsunami. Of particular interest was "karma" or "sins of a previous life." Outcomes examined included PTSD symptoms. Results indicated that belief in karma did not significantly influence PTSD symptoms after adjusting for pessimistic explanatory style (which karma was unrelated to) and other multiple other covariates including demographic factors, magnitude of exposure, social support, baseline health, depressive symptoms, and whether or not participant had received counseling. However, belief in karma *increased* risk of poor self-related health by nearly threefold (2.78, 95% CI= 1.69-4.55, p<0.0001). For a review of Buddhist practices used to recover in the aftermath of tsunamis, see Falk (2010).

Anxiety, Depression, and Suicide
Worry/anxiety. In order to compare Buddhist and Christian older adults on worry/anxiety and examine the relationship between religiosity and mental health in each group, Tapanya and colleagues (1997) surveyed 52 Christian elders (ages 65-90 years) in Canada and 52 Buddhist elders in northern Thailand (ages 65-89 years). This is one of the first studies (if not the first) to examine the relationship between religiosity and mental health in Buddhists. The Penn State Worry Questionnaire (PSWQ) was used to assess worry/anxiety, and the 20-item Gorsuch-Venable Intrinsic-Extrinsic Religiosity (IE) scale assessed religiosity. The words church, God, Bible were modified for Buddhists in the Thai version of the IE scale. After controlling for gender, results indicated no difference between Christian and Buddhist elders on PSWQ score. Buddhists scored significantly higher on extrinsic religiosity (ER) than Christians,

whereas there was little difference between groups on intrinsic religiosity (IR). An inverse relationship was found between intrinsic religiosity and worry (semi-partial r=-0.24, p<0.01) in the combined sample. This was especially true in Buddhists (r=-0.37, p<0.01). ER, on the other hand, was positively related to worry in Buddhists (r=0.29, p<0.05), but not in Christians. Investigators hypothesized that the positive relationship between ER and worry in Buddhists was because interest in the extrinsic aspects of religion may create more worry because of basic Buddhist beliefs. Whereas redemption and forgiveness for one's actions is possible in Christianity, the law of karma in Buddhism does not allow escape from the consequences of one's actions (where there is no help from a savior). For Buddhists, only perseverance toward enlightenment will bring liberation and redemption from the cycle of death and rebirth. Thus, greater extrinsic religious behavior related to activities at church/temple might not help to alleviate responsibilities for one's actions or relieve guilt in Buddhists. Among the things that each group worried about, church or temple was ranked #2 among the six greatest worries among Buddhists, but was not listed among the six greatest worries among Christians.

Depression. Limlomwongse and Liabsuetrakul (2006) followed a cohort of 610 pregnant Thai women (88.2% Buddhist) from prior to delivery until 6 to 8 weeks postpartum examining depressive symptoms. Participants were recruited from the University Hospital in South Thailand. The prevalence of significant depressive symptoms (assessed by the Edinburgh Postnatal Depression Scale) was 20.5% during pregnancy and 16.8% on the postpartum follow-up. Predictors of change in depressive symptoms included demographics, obstetric history, previous psychological problems, planned/unplanned pregnancy, perception of pregnancy complications, and other attitudes towards pregnancy and delivery. After controlling for these predictors using logistic regression, non-Buddhists were over twice as likely to experience significant depressive symptoms on follow-up compared to Buddhists (OR=2.1, 95% CI 1.0-4.0, p=0.03). This effect emerged after controlling for negative attitudes towards pregnancy.

Yeager and colleagues (2006) analyzed data from the Survey of Health and Living Status of the Elderly in Taiwan, a random sample of 2930 community-dwelling adults aged 50 or over. Relationships between religious involvement and health were assessed, including depressive symptoms (CESD). Religious affiliation of participants was Taoist/traditional folk religion (50%), Buddhist (28%), none (15%), and other religion (8%). Religious involvement was assessed using a number of measures including frequency of religious attendance at temple or church; belief in heaven/hell, existence of a living spirit after death, existence of life after death, and belief that then afterlife is better than now; and frequency of six religious practices: (1) pray/burn incense, (2) worship gods/Buddha at home, (3) read scriptures, (4) watch/listen to religious programs, (5) pray to "Lord, gods, or Buddha," and (6) ask for guidance from "Lord, gods, or Buddha" before important decisions. After controlling for baseline depression and 16 other predictors, regression analyses indicated no relationship between religious affiliation (Taoist/traditional, Buddhist, Other, or none), religious attendance, religious beliefs, or religious practices and depressive symptoms on 4-year follow-up.

Suicide. In our systematic review of quantitative studies published prior to 2010, we identified four studies that examined religiosity and suicidal thoughts, attempts or completed suicide. All four studies were conducted in China. In a study of 320 college students in China and 452 college students in U.S., Zhang and Jin (1996) examined the relationship in each group between religiosity and suicidal thoughts. Religiosity was assessed by religious attendance, private religious activities, self-rated religiosity, and religious belief. Controlling for multiple other predictors, while religiosity was significantly associated with fewer suicidal thoughts in U.S. students, it was associated with more suicidal thoughts in Chinese students.

In a case-control study, Zhang and colleagues (2004) examined risk factors for suicide (including religious beliefs) among 66 consecutive completed suicides in rural China compared to 66 controls matched on age, gender, and living location. Two informants were used to collect information from for each case of suicide (completed within past 12 months). Religious beliefs were assessed by having a religion (yes vs. no), belief in God, and belief in an afterlife. Most participants had no religion (86% cases, 96% of controls), although Buddhism and Taoism are the two largest religious groups in China. Controlling for other suicide risk factors, researchers found no difference on any of the three indicators of religious belief between completed suicides and controls.

In another case-control study, this time involving 74 urban suicide attempters and 92 controls in Northeast China, Zhang and colleagues (2006) compared self-rated religiosity and religious affiliation between cases and controls. Most participants had no religious affiliation and described their religiosity as none or weak. Of participants with a religious affiliation, two-thirds (65.2%) were Buddhist. Religious affiliation and self-rated religiosity did not significantly differ between cases and controls. In the same study, Zhang and Xu (2007) examined relationships between religious affiliation and self-rated religiosity and degree of suicide intent among suicide attempters. A Chinese version of the 8-item Beck Suicidal Intent Scale assessed suicidal intent. Suicide intent in women was significantly higher in those who were more religious (p=0.02), and a similar but weaker association was found in men (p=0.09). However, after controlling for age, mental disorder, superstition, perceived gender inequality, and marital status, these differences became non-significant.

Thus, of four studies identified here, three found no association and one reported a significant positive association between religiosity and suicidal thoughts, attempts or completions.

Substance Use/Abuse

Assanangkornchai and colleagues (2002) examined differences in religious beliefs and practices among (a) 91 alcohol-dependent persons, (b) 77 hazardous/harmful drinkers, and (c) 144 non/infrequent drinkers (controls) in Thailand. Participants were recruited from inpatient and outpatient settings, and from hospital personnel, friends, and relatives. Note that Thailand is second only to Cambodia in countries with the highest percentage Buddhist (nearly 90%). No difference was found between the three groups in terms of having been raised in a religious family, religiosity of parents, parent participation in religious activities, having religion forced on them as a child, or participation in religious activities as a child. Men without alcohol problems, however, were currently more likely than hazardous/harmful or alcohol dependent men to perceive themselves as moderately or strongly religious (86% vs. 74% and 75%, respectively), more likely to indicate Thai men should observe the Fifth Precept (i.e., avoidance of distilled or fermented intoxicants causing carelessness) (28% vs. 8% and 14%), and more likely to say that one should always abstain from drinking on a holy day (35% vs. 13% and 9%). When analyses were adjusted for age, marital status, education, working status, social class and area of residence, the strongest predictors of being a hazardous/harmful drinker and alcohol dependent were self-perception as moderately or strongly religious (OR=0.41, 95% CI=0.20-0.86, and OR=0.48, 95% CI=0.24-0.97, respectively), belief that religious teaching always influences daily life (OR=0.30, 95% CI=0.14-0.83, and OR=0.50, 95% CI=0.21-1.06), and interest in studying the Buddha's teachings (OR=0.51, 95% CI=0.28-0.93, and OR=0.81, 95% CI=0.47-1.41). However, those serving as a "temple boy" as a child were more likely to be alcohol dependent (OR=2.04, 95% CI=1.14-3.61). The authors explained that temple boys live together as a group in a dormitory, and have fewer restrictions and greater opportunity to use alcohol.

Psychological Well-being/Life Satisfaction
Kim (2003) examined the relationship between religious involvement and psychological well-being in South Korea, where 23% are Buddhist, 20% are Protestant, 7% are Catholic, and 49% have no affiliation (according to the 1995 Korean National Statistical Office survey cited in this report). Kim analyzed data from a random sample of 1,613 adults by Gallup Korea in 1997, which included information on religious affiliation and life satisfaction. Life satisfaction was assessed on a scale from 1 (low) to 10 (high). Uncontrolled analyses revealed that life satisfaction was highest in Protestants (6.5), then Catholics (6.4), then those with no religious affiliation (5.9), and finally Buddhists (5.8). The author points out that this may have been due to differences in education and income, since Korean Buddhists have less education than Catholics or Protestants.

In a study of social capital, Yamaoka (2008) analyzed data from a random sample of 8,665 adults living in Japan, South Korea, Singapore, five cities in China, and Taiwan, examining relationships between religious faith and life satisfaction, somatic symptoms, and self-rated health. Religious faith (without description) was assessed using a single item that was dichotomized for analysis (present vs.

absent). Religious faith was present in 24-25% of participants in Japan, 7-27% in China, 26-41% in Hong Kong, 71- 78% in Taiwan, 76-82% in Singapore, and 43-50% in South Korea. Logistic regression models were used to analyze the data controlling for other predictors. Religious faith was associated with a *higher number* of somatic symptoms (OR=1.35, 95% CI 1.21-1.51) and *poorer* subjective health (OR=1.14, 95% CI 1.01-1.29), but there was no relationship with life satisfaction (OR=1.03, 95% CI 0.89-1.19).

Quality of Life/Self-Rated Health

In one of the first studies comparing Buddhists and non-Buddhists on mental health, Fazel and Young (1988) examined the quality of life of 59 Tibetan refugees (Mahayana Buddhists) and 66 native Hindus in Northern India. Quality of life was assessed using 17-items taken from the Perceived Quality of Life inventory (Andrews & Withey). Results indicated that quality of life was significantly higher among Buddhist Tibetan refugees compared to native Hindus (p<0.001, uncontrolled). This was especially true among the "laborers" class (in contrast to the shopkeepers class, where no differences in QOL were observed). Researchers concluded that "While both Hindus and Tibetans subscribe to the fatalistic attitude of Karma, the Tibetans report greater life satisfaction. If one looks beyond the superficial similarities in the concept of Karma, however, it becomes clear that Tibetans adopt a 'proactive' posture as opposed to the 'reactive' fatalism of the Hindus" (p. 229). Explaining what "proactive" means, researchers indicated that Buddhists emphasize aspects of daily life that help them gain positive karma, whereas Hindus find reasons for their misfortunes in their karma.

With regard to self-rated health (known to be heavily influenced by mental health), Krause and colleagues (1999) analyzed data from a national probability survey of 2,153 older adults in Japan, examining relationships between religious activity, self-rated physical health (SRH), and altruism (helping others). Most Japanese are Shinto, but approximately three quarters also practice Buddhism. Average age of participants was 70 years (56% women, 69% married, mean education level 10 years). With regard to private religious practices, 80% sometimes or always participated in prayers and offerings to ancestors; one-third sometimes or always read scriptures (Buddhist scriptures or the Bible); and 18% sometimes or always watched or listened to religious programs on TV or radio. Altruism ("support provided to others") was assessed with two questions that asked about frequency of listening to others talk about their troubles, and frequency of encouraging and comforting those undergoing hardships. SRH was assessed using a 3-item index. Results indicated that greater religious practice among men (but not women) was associated with more altruistic activities. Religious practice was associated with better SRH in both men and women. The effect of religious practice on health in men was mediated (explained) largely by providing support to others (altruism).

Personality Traits

Saroglou & Dupuis (2006) examined the relationship between personality characteristics, cognitive structure, importance of values, and religiosity in 105 Buddhists living in Belgium. Participants were recruited from Buddhist centers in Belgium belonging to the Tibetan Vajrayana tradition. Psychological characteristics assessed were need for closure (preference for order, predictability, decisiveness, discomfort from ambiguity, closemindedness), agreeableness (kind, sympathetic, cooperative, warm and considerate), and "values" using standard measures of these constructs. Religiosity was assessed using a 14-item Investment in Buddhism Scale (IBS) developed by the authors that included frequency of practice (both collective and individual), self-identification as Buddhist, interest in Buddhism, finding a way of life through Buddhism, working on oneself in Buddhism, and willingness to share Buddhism with others and their children. In addition, religious quest was assessed using the Quest scale (Altemeyer & Hunsberger). Results indicated that "need for closure" and "closemindedness" were inversely associated with Buddhist collective religious practice, and Buddhist "inner directed-ness" was inversely associated with preference for predictability. All measures of Buddhist religiosity on the IBS were associated with high scores on agreeableness. IBS also tended to be positively associated with preference for tradition, conformity universalism, and benevolence, but was negatively correlated with need for security, power, achievement, and hedonism (especially).

Buddhist Interventions

There have been many, many studies of mindfulness meditation (or

Mindfulness Based Stress Reduction, MBSR) largely conducted in Western countries and in non-Buddhists. The results of these studies have been summarized in a series of meta-analyses or systematic reviews reported both before 2010 (Grossman et al., 2004; Weaver et al., 2008; Chiesa & Serretti, 2009) and after 2010 (Kuyken et al., 2016; Spijkerman et al., 2016).

We focus here, though, on interventions specifically focused on Buddhist beliefs and practices usually conducted in Buddhist populations. This is primarily because of the "huge differences between the Western and Eastern approaches" (Schmidt, 2011, p 23) that result from Western mindfulness being largely stripped of its religious components (i.e., the Eightfold Path, particularly the first five moral precepts).

Emavardhana and Tori (1997) tested the effects of Vipassana meditation on psychological adjustment among two cohorts of 222 and 216 young Thai persons (average age 18 years), compared to a young adult Thai control group (n=281). Vipassana meditation is one of the oldest forms of Buddhist meditation that developed within the Theravada tradition. Similar to mindfulness meditation, it involves mindful observation of whatever arises in consciousness. Participants in the first two cohorts attended a seven-day Vipassana meditation retreat as part of activities supported by the Young Buddhist Association of Thailand. Each day was similar and began a 4:00 AM. Complete silence was observed at all times. All activities including eating and walking were done in a state of heightened awareness. The day was spent with alternating periods of sitting and walking meditation, mindfulness exercises, listening to brief sermons, and performing morning and evening prayers. Small group discussions were also held with the meditation master. The day ended with an hour of sitting meditation and evening chanting. Controls and meditating groups were similar in age, gender, education, percent high school students, and demographics, but controls received no intervention of any kind. Both groups completed test forms before and after the seven-day retreat or observation period. Results indicated that compared to controls, meditators after the retreat scored higher on self-concept, positive ego defense mechanisms, maturity, tolerance of common stressors, and Buddhist beliefs and practices. Buddhist beliefs and practices were associated with greater self-esteem and less impulsiveness.

Tori (1999) compared the effects of attending a 3-day Roman Catholic retreat (n=102), a 3-day Buddhist retreat (n=102), or a control condition (n=102) in 306 teenage Thai girls (average age 16 years). Thai girls in the Roman Catholic retreat group were from a large parochial high school in Bangkok. Participants attending the Buddhist retreat were part of the Young Buddhist Association of Thailand or were from elsewhere in the country. Those in the control group attended government secondary schools in Bangkok. The Adjective Checklist was used to compare the emotional state of girls before and after the retreat (emotional maturity, achievement, sympathetic warmth) with controls. The Catholic retreat involved liturgical ceremonies, prayer, sermons, and discussion groups. In contrast, the Buddhist retreat involved complete silence, alternating periods of sitting and walking meditation, a sermon, and paying respect to Buddha. Results indicated that Thai girls attending the Buddhist retreat showed significantly greater change scores on emotional maturity and sympathetic warmth (but not achievement) compared to Thai girls attending the Catholic retreat or those in the control condition.

Margolin and colleagues (2006) examined the efficacy of a spiritually-focused intervention for improving motivation for HIV prevention among 72 non-Asian methadone-maintained patients in New Haven, CT. All participants (ages 21-56) were opiate dependent using heroin for an average of 17.7 years prior to entering the methadone treatment program. They were randomized to either standard care plus eight weeks of the intervention (n=38) or standard care alone (n=34). The intervention was 3-S Therapy, which authors described as a manual-guided spiritually-focused psychotherapy using a Buddhist framework (the Eightfold Path). In this study, the 3-S therapy was administered in eight weekly sessions, either as individual sessions (n=20) or as group therapy sessions (n=18). Measures administered at baseline and post-treatment (2 time points) were a computerized reaction time task, spiritual/religious practices (four items assessing private religious practices and two items measuring public religious practices), a measure of the 10 Buddhist perfections, measures of motivation for HIV prevention and HIV risk behavior, and a qualitative posttreatment interview. Eighty-five percent of participants completed the 8-week study. Computerized reaction time, spiritual/religious practice, expression of spiritual qualities in daily life, and motivation for HIV prevention increased and HIV risk behaviors decreased from baseline to follow-up in the intervention group (with all time by group interactions significant at p<0.05).

Rungreangkulkij and Wongtakee (2008) examined the effects of Buddhist counseling in 21 participants with anxiety disorder in northeastern Thailand (average age 42, all Buddhists). Buddhist counseling (administered by a graduate nursing student) was based on the "three universal natural laws": the law of impermanence (anicca), the law of suffering (dukka), and the law of selfishness or no self (detachment from the physical world and the ego) (anatta). Assessed were anxiety symptoms using the State-Trait Anxiety Inventory (STAI). Each session lasted 60-90 minutes and was organized into four stages: (1) developing rapport, active listening, and demonstrating compassion; (2) education using stories and explaining the universal natural laws; (3) practicing mindfulness meditation during the session (and at home); and (4) conclusion and assessment of participants' perceptions, beliefs and understanding. A total of two sessions were held separated by one month. Participants were assessed at baseline, post-intervention, and at 2 month follow-up with the STAI administered by a nurse (the same nurse doing the counseling?). After the three-month period STAI scores decreased significantly (p<0.001). Investigators concluded that the study indicated that counseling based on Buddhist principles had the potential to benefit patients with anxiety disorders.

Summary

The above reports are the only studies published prior to 2010 that could be located in our systematic exhaustive review of the literature (Koenig et al., 2012). There were 22 observational studies and 4 clinical trials. Five of the 22 observational studies were descriptive or qualitative, suggesting that Buddhist beliefs and practices are used widely to cope with psychological stressors. Five quantitative studies compared Buddhists and non-Buddhists, with three finding that Buddhists had better mental health than non-Buddhists, one finding worse mental health (likely due to lower educational and income level), and one finding no difference. The remaining 12 studies examined the association between religiosity and mental health among Buddhist population (or Asian populations with a large proportion of Buddhists). Of those, four (33%) reported positive associations with better mental health or fewer suicidal tendencies, three indicated a negative association (25%), one reported mixed results (positive with intrinsic religiosity, negative with extrinsic religiosity), and four found no association. While all four intervention studies described above showed significant effects, the methods were limited by either having no comparison control group or the control group did not receive a comparable amount of social attention as the intervention group. Thus, the benefits found for these interventions may have been due to higher levels of social contact and attention or simply due to the passage of time.

These studies suggest that the mental health of Buddhists is as good as (if not better than) that of non-Buddhists, that religious practice among Buddhists is sometimes (four of twelve studies) associated with better mental health and perceptions of health, and that Buddhist-based intervention are frequently effective in reducing distressing emotional symptoms in Buddhists compared to no treatment.

Conclusions

This systematic review of quantitative (and some qualitative) research conducted up through 2010 examined studies that compared Buddhists and non-Buddhists on mental health (and substance use), explored the relationship between religiosity and mental health in Buddhists, and examined the effects of Buddhist interventions on mental health outcomes. These early studies suggest that Buddhists often have better mental health than non-Buddhists (especially in situations of high stress or torture). Buddhist beliefs/practices are sometimes associated with better mental health and sometimes with worse mental health. Buddhist interventions uniformly lead to a reduction in symptoms of mental distress (at least among studies reviewed here. Limitations in research methodology, however, prevent any definitive conclusions in this regard. What about more recent research?

CHAPTER 7

LATEST RESEARCH

Presented in this chapter are selected recent studies that have been chosen to illustrate the type of research now being reported in the literature. These studies are again reported in categories of mental health outcome: coping with stress, depression and anxiety, alcohol and drug use/abuse, psychological well-being, quality of life, personality traits, and studies of Buddhist interventions. The chapter ends with unpublished original research that (1) compares the mental health and well-being of Buddhists with that of those with other religious affiliation (Christian, Muslim, Hindu, etc.) and those with no religious affiliation, and (2) examines associations between religiosity and well-being in Buddhists using data from large national and cross-national surveys conducted primarily in East Asia.

Several quantitative scales measuring Buddhist beliefs/practice have been developed over the past 10 years, greatly facilitating future research in this area. Besides the 11-item Buddhist Beliefs and Practices Scale (Emavardhana & Tori, 1997) discussed in the last chapter, those newer scales include the 66-item Buddhist COPE that assesses 14 types of Buddhist coping behaviors (Phillips et al., 2012); the 30-item Measure of Nonattachment that examines grasping or clinging behavior among Buddhists (Sahdra et al., 2010); and the 24-item Scale of Attitude toward Buddhism that measures positive and negative beliefs about Buddhism (Thanissaro, 2011). Although not used often, these are tools that researchers may use in the future to quantify Buddhist belief and activity in order to examine relationships with mental health outcomes. Caution, though, is needed when using these scales since, as with other spirituality scales, many of the items on these scales include indicators of positive mental health, resulting in measurement contamination and tautological, un-interpretable relationships with mental health outcomes (Koenig, 2008; Tsuang & Simpson, 2008; MacDonald, 2017). Fortunately, most studies described below did not use these scales, instead choosing specific Buddhist beliefs and practices in order to examine their relationship to mental health.

Coping with Stress

Cook and Hayes (2010) surveyed 154 Asian American and 154 Caucasian American college students at the University of California, Davis, comparing coping styles between the groups: (a) acceptance of emotions and willingness to take action (Hays et al.'s Acceptance and Action Questionnaire), (b) resignation acceptance due to fate (Resignation Acceptance Questionnaire), (c) tendency to suppress unwanted thoughts (Bear Suppression Inventory), and (d) attempts to control unwanted thoughts (Thought Control Questionnaire). Psychological health was measured by the Fear of Sadness Scale and Symptom Check List-90-R. Results indicated that Asian American students scored significantly lower than Caucasian students on psychological acceptance, but significantly higher on resignation acceptance. Negative psychological symptoms (indicated by a score of 65 or higher on the SCL-90-R) were also significantly higher among Asian American students (63%) compared to Caucasian students (34%). Asian Buddhists (n=27) were not more psychologically healthy than Asian Christians (n=72) nor were there any differences in psychological coping styles (Buddhists were not more self-accepting despite Buddhist teachings). Among Asian Buddhists, frequency of religious practice was not correlated with greater psychological acceptance.

Falb and Pargament (2013) surveyed 92 Buddhist end-of-life caregivers in the U.S. identified through contemplative caregiver training programs and a Buddhist chaplaincy listserv. Participants were 89% Caucasian, 78% with post-graduate degrees, and 67% female. Caregiver identities were 29% clergy, 25% medical professional, 20% volunteer, and 19% family or friend. The purpose was to identify positive and negative Buddhist coping behaviors and their relationship to spiritual well-being (SWB) (assessed by the FACIT-Sp), burnout (Maslach Burnout Inventory, MBI), depression (CESD), and posttraumatic growth (PTG Inventory). Phillips et al's 66-item Buddhist COPE was used to assess Buddhist coping behaviors. Controlled for in analyses were number of months of caregiving, age, self-rated spirituality, months meditating, and participation in a contemplative caregiver training program. Regression analyses identified independent correlations between the 14 Buddhist coping subscales and 7 mental health outcomes (a total of 98 analyses). Results indicated significant associations between BCOPE subscales and mental health outcomes: BCOPE "morality" subscale with lower MBI depersonalization (B=-0.35) and greater PTG (B=0.37); the BCOPE "mindfulness" subscale and greater SWB (B=0.36); the BCOPE "dharma" subscale and lower PTG (B=-0.40); the BCOPE "impermanence" subscale and both less MBI exhaustion (B=-0.37) and greater PTG (B=0.38); the BCOPE "inter being" subscale and greater MBI exhaustion (B=0.44); the BCOPE "not self" subscale and less MBI exhaustion (B=-0.36); and especially the BCOPE "bad Buddhist" subscale and greater MBI exhaustion (B=0.34), lower SWB (B=-0.19), and higher CESD (B=0.33). No other significant relationships (p<0.05) were found between individual BCOPE subscales and mental health outcomes. Overall, then, positive BCOPE subscales were associated with less burnout and greater spiritual well-being, whereas negative BCOPE subscales were correlated with less SWB and greater depression.

Anxiety, Depression and Suicide

Phillips et al (2012)'s original validation study of the BCOPE examined associations with mental health outcomes in 869 non-Asian Buddhists in the U.S. (39% Mahayana, 34% Varayana, 21% Theravada). Participants were 55% female, average age 46 years, and 87% Caucasian. Associations between BCOPE subscales, anxiety and depression were examined, after controlling for demographic and general spiritual characteristics (i.e., years practicing Buddhism and self-rated spirituality). The BCOPE "bad Buddhist" subscale (wished could stop judging self; forced things instead of accepting them) was associated with greater anxiety and greater depression; the "fatalistic karma" subscale (felt powerless since karma caused event; helpless since situation due to karmic past) with more depression; and the "impermanence" subscale (reminded self that stress would pass; recognized all things change) with less depression (all p<0.001).

In the validation study of the Nonattachment Scale (conducted in U.S. college students), Sahdra et al., 2010 also found moderately strong inverse associations between nonattachment scores and both depression (r=-0.27, p<0.01) and anxiety (r=-0.35, p<0.01). As indicated earlier, some of the positive relationships reported in both the Phillips et al and Sahdra et al studies are likely due to inclusion of items assessing positive mental health constructs in these Buddhist scales.

Death anxiety. Hui and Coleman (2012) surveyed 141 older adults Hong Kong Chinese Buddhists to examine the relationship between reincarnation beliefs and death anxiety, hypothesizing that belief in reincarnation would protect from death anxiety. Chinese Buddhists age 55 or older who had taken the Three Refuges (Buddha, Buddha Dharma, and Sangha) were eligible to participate. Approximately half of the sample was ages 55-59 years old, 68% were female, 62% were married, and 57% were retired. Reincarnation beliefs were assessed using an 8-item Buddhist Reincarnation Beliefs Scale, which assessed belief in karma as the determinant of the next rebirth, reincarnation as imprisonment, and the possibility of transcending reincarnation. The 15-item Chinese Death Anxiety Scale was used to assess anxiety surrounding death and dying. Results indicated that participants had on average a strong belief in reincarnation and a low level of personal death anxiety. However, no association was found between reincarnation belief and death anxiety either in the overall sample or the sample dichotomized by age group. Researchers hypothesize that the lack of relationship might be because "Buddhists view reincarnation not as a solace but rather as a renewal of sufferings due to unwholesome karma" (p 949).

Wong and colleagues (2015) surveyed 123 Christians and 137 Buddhists (matched on demographic characteristics) living in Hong Kong, comparing the two groups on religiosity and death attitudes. Adults (ages 18 to 80) were invited by their religious congregations to fill out a questionnaire; response rates were 94% for Buddhists and 77% for Christians. Religiosity was assessed with the 14-item Intrinsic/Extrinsic-Revised Scale (I/E-R), and death attitudes by the 32-item Revised Collett-Lester Fear of Death and Dying Scale and by the 32-item Death Attitude Profile-Revised Scale (DAP-R). Also measured were stressful life events within the past two years (death of close friend or relative, serious illness of close friend or relative, or presence of serious life-threatening illness), current physical illnesses, mental health (General Health Questionnaire), and demographics (age, education, etc.). Regardless of religion, higher levels of intrinsic religiosity (religion as an end in its self) were associated with lower levels of fear of death and dying, and higher levels of death acceptance. Likewise, regardless of religion, extrinsic religiosity (religion as a means to achieve other ends) was associated with greater fear of death and dying. Christians scored higher on fear of death and dying then Buddhists, although differences were small (2.96 vs. 2.85, p<0.05). Extrinsic religiosity was unrelated to death acceptance for Christians but significantly predicted death acceptance and death avoidance in Buddhists. Thus, more extrinsically religious Buddhists were more likely to accept death and to avoid death. Researchers concluded that intrinsic religiosity protected both Buddhists and Christians from fear of death and helped them to accept death, although attributed differences in the belief systems of Buddhists and Christians to explain the associations with extrinsic religiosity among Buddhists (note however the difference in these findings and those of Tapanya and colleagues (1997) discussed in the last chapter).

Depression. Roemer (2010a) analyzed data from a random sample of 600 Japanese adults living in the Kyoto Prefecture, examining the relationship between religious beliefs and depressive symptoms in this largely Shinto-Buddhist population (over the years, Shintoism and Mahayana Buddhism in Japan have become closely interwoven). Religious involvement was assessed by a 6-item Religious Coping Index (RCI) (i.e., religion provides comfort and peace, praying purifies me, kami-hotoke helps me, kami-hotoke gives aid, kami-hotoke protects me, kami-hotoke curses people). Also assessed were ownership of a household ancestor alter (Butsudan) or Shinto shrine (kamidana), frequency of rituals conducted there, frequency of visits to ancestral grave-sites, belief in the existence of kami or hotoke, importance of respecting ancestors, and religiousness (belief that "faith [shinko] and religiousness [shukyoteki na koto] are important for mental and physical health"). Depressive symptoms were assessed with the 10-item Japanese CESD. After controlling for socio-demographic variables and health characteristics, RCI score (religious coping) was *positively* related to depressive symptoms (B=0.12, p<0.01). Ownership of a Shinto altar was also positively associated with depression (B=0.07, p<0.05), as was belief in the existence of kami (gods, deities, spirits) and hotoke (ancestors, buddhas) (B=0.13, p<0.01) and belief that ancestors should be respected (B=0.15, p<0.001). The only religious characteristics inversely related to depression were ownership of an ancestor altar and frequency of making ancestor grave site visits (both B=-0.16, p<0.01). Religiousness was not associated with depression. Roemer concluded that: "Overall, there is strong evidence that certain dimensions of religiousness are associated with well-being in Japan, and as the results of this study revealed, these connections are mainly harmful" (p 579). This statement, however, goes considerably beyond what can be said from these cross-sectional data.

Xue and colleagues (2016) at the Ragama Rheumatology and Rehabilitation Hospital in Sri Lanka surveyed 61 inpatients (85% Buddhist) with traumatic spinal cord injury (SCI). Measures included the SCI Independence Scale, the 6-item Benefit through Spirituality/ Religiosity Scale, Sheehan Disability Inventory, and Beck Depression Inventory (BDI). Linear regression was used to examine predictors of depressive symptoms, controlling for sociodemographic variables. Over 40% of participants scored in the significant depression range of the BDI. The only predictors of depressive symptoms were degree of impairment in physical functioning (β=0.54, p<0.001) and benefit through S/R activities (β=-0.31, p<0.05). Researchers concluded that "The findings emphasize the need for rehabilitative programing to support patients' S/R activities and mental well-being, promoting reintegration into their community roles" (p. 1158).

Suicide. I was able to locate eight reports published since 2010 on religion and suicide in Buddhist majority countries (or where Buddhism was the majority religion among those affiliated with a religion). Three reports involved cross-national studies, and of the other five studies, all five were conducted in China. In the first cross-national study, Stack and Kposowa (2011) analyzed data from a random sample of over 50,000 people participating in the World Values Survey, Wave 4, finding that suicide acceptability was significantly lower in Buddhists than in those with no religious affiliation (B=-0.181, p<0.01), a finding that persisted after controlling for religiosity and numerous demographic controls. However, in a later analysis of WVS Wave 4 data (using a smaller sample of 42,299), no association was found with suicide acceptability either (a) at the individual level between Buddhist affiliation and no affiliation or (b) at the country level (percentage Buddhist) (Boyd & Chung, 2012).

The other cross-national study by Peltzer and colleagues (2017) surveyed 4,675 undergraduate students in Cambodia, Indonesia, Malaysia, Myanmar, Thailand and Vietnam, examining likelihood of ever having suicidal ideation or made a suicide attempt. Three-quarters of the sample were from Buddhist-majority countries. Overall, those with higher organizational religiosity (attending religious services) were significantly less likely to have experienced suicidal ideation, although no difference was found for any measure of religious involvement and suicide attempt.

In the first of the five studies conducted in mainland China, Li and Phillips (2010) surveyed 629 college students along with other community groups in Eastern China. In the college student sample, researchers assessed presence of religious belief (yes vs. no), and if yes, asked about religious affiliation (35 of 48 students with a religious affiliation were Buddhist). Acceptability of suicide was measured using a 25-item scale assessing the acceptability of suicide in a variety of situations. Presence of religious belief (any) was associated with *increased* acceptability of suicide.

Wang and colleagues (2015) examined suicidal ideation and behavior in a population-based sample of 2,769 community-dwelling adults in Western China, finding no association between religious affiliation and suicidal thoughts or behaviors. Likewise, Zou and colleagues (2016) surveyed a representative sample of 983 urban and rural adults from northeastern China, finding that religious belief was again unrelated to attitudes toward suicide. Hong and colleagues (2016) surveyed 15,957 adults age 60 years or older from across China; religiosity was assessed by asking respondents if they were religious and then if yes, what their religious affiliation was. Results indicated that Christians (17% of the sample) were more likely than those with no religious affiliation to attempt suicide in last 12 months. However, there were no differences in suicidal thoughts or attempts between Buddhists (34.3% of the sample, i.e., the most common religious group) and those with no religious affiliation.

Sun and Zhang (2017) compared 791 medically serious suicide attempters with 791 controls aged 15-54 years in rural areas of North and South China, finding that religious belief was somewhat more common among male suicide attempters; however, once other risk factors were taken into account, the difference in religious belief decreased to non-significance. Specific religious affiliation was not given.

Thus, the overall trend is no association between religious belief and suicidal ideation in Buddhist-majority samples (5 of 8 studies), although one study found increased acceptability of suicide and two other studies found decreased suicidal ideation or suicide acceptability (both cross-national studies). In conclusion, more recent studies generally find little relationship between religiosity and suicidal ideation, attempts, or acceptability in Buddhists (despite theoretical considerations that might anticipate higher suicide rates or acceptability in Buddhists).

Alcohol and Drug Use/Abuse

Chamratrithirong and colleagues (2010) surveyed a random sample of 420 pairs of parents and teens from the Bangkok (Thailand) metropolitan area to examine the effects of family spiritual beliefs/ practices on substance use and sexual behaviors of adolescents ages 13-14 years. Data were utilized from the 2007 Thai Family Matters Project. Buddhist spiritual beliefs in adolescents and parents were assessed by "perception of the importance of religion to self" (44% of adolescents indicating "a lot"), "belief in the help of religious prayer or meditation" (31%), and "belief in reincarnation and in the law of karma" (25% for belief in reincarnation and 47% for belief in karma). Buddhist spiritual practices were assessed by "regular religious prayer or meditation" (34%), "religious prayer or meditation when life is stressful" (14%), "practices of merit making including Tamboon (donation) and Saihart (offering food to monks)" (7%), and "observation of the Five Precepts including abstinence from killing, stealing, sexual misconduct, lying, and substance use" (10%). Results indicated that spiritual beliefs and practices (SBP) of teens were not related to alcohol use once parental monitoring and age were controlled for. However, parent (but not teen) spiritual beliefs (B=-0.057, p<0.05) and practices (B=-0.063, p<0.05) were related indirectly to lower cigarette smoking. Neither parent nor teen SBP were related to sexual intention; however, concerning pre-sexual behaviors, parents' spiritual beliefs (B=-0.044, p<0.001), parents' spiritual practices (B=-0.041, p<0.01), and teens' spiritual beliefs (B=-0.079, p<0.01) were indirectly and inversely related, and teen spiritual practices were directly and inversely related (B=-0.14, p<0.01).

Wongtongkam et al (2014) examined a sample of 1,778 Thai adolescents (97% male) attending public technical colleges in Bangkok (capital city of Thailand) and Nakhon Ratchasima (rural province). Religiosity was assessed as one of 12 peer/individual domains possibly influencing alcohol or drug use. Again, higher religious involvement was associated with a 38% decreased risk of using alcoholic beverages, after adjusting for age, gender, grade completed, enrollment department, daily income, and family income (OR=0.62, 95% CI 0.41-0.95). Religiosity was not associated with other illicit drug use (sniffing glue, cocaine, marijuana, methamphet-amine, heroin, ecstasy), although the prevalence rate was low (2%).

In perhaps the methodologically most rigorous study of predictors of problematic alcohol use in a Buddhist country, Assanangkornchai and colleagues (2010) analyzed data from the Thai National Household Survey for Substance and Alcohol Use that surveyed a random national sample of 26,633 persons aged 12-65 years from across Thailand. A standard measure for assessing alcohol use (the AUDIT) was administered to participants, 91% of whom were Buddhist. Results indicated that 63% were lifetime abstainers (i.e., never drank more than one or two alcoholic drinks in their lifetime), and 29% were current drinkers. Based on AUDIT scores, 7% were classified as moderate level problem or hazardous drinkers, 1% as high level problem or harmful drinkers, and 0.6% as very severe-level problem drinkers or probable alcohol dependence. Although level of religious involvement was not assessed, Buddhist religious affiliation was associated with a *greater likelihood* of experiencing hazardous-harmful drinking, independent of gender, age, education, marital status, occupation, household area, and region of the country (members of other religious affiliations were at significantly lower risk compared to Buddhists; adjusted OR=0.70, 95% CI 0.55-0.92).

Psychological Well-Being

Roemer (2010b) analyzed data from 14,322 participants surveyed during the 2000-2005 Japanese General Social Surveys (combined samples from these years). These are random national samples of Japanese adults. Participants were asked "Do you have a religion you believe in?" Three possible responses were "yes," "I don't really believe [in one], but I have a family religion," and "no." If yes, participants were asked their religion: Buddhism (4.5%, n=547), New Religion (3.3%, n=402), Christianity (0.9%, n=114), and other (0.9%, n=105). Somewhat surprisingly, 90.4% (n=10,957 of 12,121) indicated they had no religion in which they personally believed. All participants (n=14,186) were asked to rate their level of devotion to their religion on a scale ranging from 0 (none) to 3 (devoted). Subjective well-being was assessed by life satisfaction (0 dissatisfied to 4 satisfied) in the domains of leisure activities, family life, friendships, household income, and area of residence. Summing responses each domain resulted in a life satisfaction index ranging from 0 to 20. Happiness was measured by a single item with responses ranging from 1 (unhappy) to 5 (happy). After controlling for sociodemographic variables, health status, hobbies, social class, marital and employment status, results indicated that level of religious devotion was positively related to life satisfaction (B=0.28, p<0.001). Likewise, compared to those with no religion, Buddhists (B=0.50, p<0.01), New Religionists (B=0.37, p<0.05), and Christians (B=1.01, p<0.01) were all more likely to be satisfied with life. The same findings were noted for happiness, causing the researcher to conclude that "...this study reveals that religious devotion and affiliation with certain religions are positively and significantly correlated with life satisfaction and happiness in Japan" (p 411). These results (and conclusion) are quite different from the Roemer (2010a) report on religion and depression in Japan summarized earlier.

Liu and colleagues (2012) examined the association between religious involvement and happiness in a random sample of 1,881 adults living in Taiwan who participated in the Taiwan Social Change Survey. Average age of participants was 43 years, 40% were female, 62% were married, and religious affiliations were Buddhist (24%),

Taoist (16%), popular religion (30%), Christian (4%), other religion (6%), and no religion (20%). Religious involvement was assessed by frequency of religious attendance (responses 1-8, average 3.2), making an offering during a pilgrimage (16% yes), worshiping God(s) and ancestral spirits (85% yes), Buddhist chanting (9% yes), reading religious scriptures (8% yes), practicing Qigong (1% yes), sitting in meditation (5%), giving thanks, repenting or praying every day (yes=4%), belief in a supreme God (responses 1-4, average 2.6), and belief in the laws of karma (responses 1-4, average 3.1). Happiness was measured by a single item that range from 1 (very unhappy) to 4 (very happy). After controlling for health-related stress (the strongest correlate of happiness) and demographics, the religious practice of "giving thanks, repenting, or praying every day" was associated with greater happiness (B=0.18, p<0.05), whereas belief in "a supreme God in the universe" was associated with *less happiness* (B=-0.05, p<0.05). No other religious characteristics were associated with happiness. However, there was an interaction between belief in a supreme God and health-related stress, such that among those with health problems, stronger belief in a supreme God was associated with *greater happiness* (B=0.10, p<0.01). Given that Buddhists made up only 24% of the sample, it is not known whether this finding was also present in the Buddhist subgroup.

Quality of Life

Khumsaen and colleagues (2012) examine predictors of quality of life (QOL) in a study of 120 people living with HIV in Thailand. Included among predictors was spiritual well-being (SWB). Participants included 62% females, and most were ages 31 to 50 years. SWB was measured using the JAREL SWB scale (Hungelmann et al). QOL was assessed by the World Health Organization QOL-BREF scale. Regression analyses controlled for age, gender, marital status, employment, education, living status, monthly income time since HIV diagnosis, and social support. SWB predicted higher levels of QOL independent of other predictors (B=0.26, p=0.004). Unfortunately, the JAREL scale (a non-Buddhist spirituality measure) is heavily contaminated with items measuring meaning and purpose in life, satisfaction with life, well-being, and acceptance of life situation, making it difficult to interpret the finding.

Moon and colleagues (2013) examined the association between

religiosity/spirituality (R/S) and QOL in 274 adults age 65 or older living alone in Chuncheon city, South Korea. The average age of participants was 77 years and 82% were women. Religious affiliations were 33% Protestant, 18% Buddhist, and 16% Catholic. The Duke Religion Index (DUREL) was used to assess religious involvement (religious attendance, private religious activity, and intrinsic religiosity). The 15-item Geriatric Depression Scale and the Geriatric Qualify of Life-Dementia scale were used to assess QOL. While religiosity (particularly intrinsic religiosity) was associated with less depression and greater QOL in Protestants and Catholics, no association was found in Buddhists (although there were only 48 Buddhists in the sample, reducing the power to detect an effect).

In one of the few longitudinal studies, Jang et al (2013) surveyed 284 Korean women with breast cancer undergoing surgery, assessing religiosity, QOL, anxiety, and depression at baseline and 12 month follow-up. The average age of participants was 50 years. Religious affiliation was 51% Christian (35% Protestants, 16% Catholics), 22% Buddhists, and 26% no religion. Religiosity was also assessed with the 5-item Duke Religion Index (combining organizational and private religious activity into a religious activity scale and combining the three intrinsic religiosity items into an IR subscale). QOL was assessed using the European Organization for the Research and Treatment of Cancer (EORTC) Quality of Life Questionnaire Core 30; depression was identified by the MINI Neuropsychiatric Inventory (combining major and minor depression for analyses) and observer-rated depressive symptoms by the Montgomery-Asbury Depression Rating Scale. Anxiety and depression were also self-assessed by the Hospital Anxiety Depression Scale (HADS). Results indicated a significant reduction in the prevalence of depressive disorder (major and minor) from baseline to follow-up among Protestants (30.1% to 15.7%, p=0.03), but no change in Buddhists (13.7% to 17.6%, p=0.77), Catholics, or non-affiliates. At baseline, there was a trend for anxiety symptoms on the HADS to be lower among Buddhists (3.0) compared to Protestants (4.0), Catholics (5.5), and those with no religion (4.0) (p<0.10, adjusted for age and education). One year after surgery, anxiety symptoms on the HADS remained somewhat lower (2.0) among Buddhists compared to other Christian groups (4.0-5.0) and those with no religion (4.0) (p=0.18). No significant differences between Buddhists, Christians, and non-affiliates at either baseline or follow-up were found on quality of life or depressive symptoms. In the overall sample, after controlling for age and education, higher intrinsic religiosity (but not religious activities) predicted greater global QOL at 12-month follow-up. Among Buddhists (n=63 at baseline, n=49 at follow-up), religious activities (but not intrinsic religiosity) was associated with fewer baseline depressive symptoms (partial r=-0.42, p<0.01), fewer follow-up anxiety symptoms at 12 months (partial r=-0.30, p<0.05), and greater follow-up global QOL (r=0.29, p<0.05) at 12 months. Researchers concluded that while religiosity influences the quality of life and emotional state of breast cancer patients in Korea, it may differ depending on type of religious affiliation.

Personality Traits

O'Connor and colleagues (2012) compared empathy-based guilt, empathic distress, having an overly active moral system, and depressive symptoms in 98 Tibetan Buddhist meditation practitioners and 438 non-Buddhist non-meditating community adults living in the United States. Tibetan Buddhist meditators (identified from a Tibetan Buddhist listserv) were 32% Mahayana, 19% Vajrayana, 8% Pure Land, and 41% other (combination of traditions). Since all Tibetan Buddhist meditators were from the U.S., most were European-American (68%) and were highly educated (16% doctorate, 30% master's degree, and 26% with college or graduate school). Only 8% were Asian. Of the 438 non-Buddhists recruited via advertisements on Craigslist, 51% were European-American, 15% Asian, and the remainder other ethnicities or mixed; only 17% had doctorates or master's degrees, and so were considerately less educated than Tibetan Buddhist meditators. Religious affiliation of non-Buddhists was not specified. Personality traits were examined with the 44-item Big Five Inventory (BFI) (neuroticism, extraversion, agreeableness, conscientiousness, and openness to experience). Guilt was measured with the 67-item Interpersonal Guilt Questionnaire (made up of survivor, separation, and omnipotent subscales); empathy was assessed by the 28-item Interpersonal Reactivity Index (made up of perspective-taking, empathic concern, and empathic distress subscales); and altruism was measured by the 45-item Compassionate Altruism Scale (made up of family, friends, and strangers subscales). Results indicated that Buddhist Tibetan meditators scored significantly lower than non-Buddhists on the omnipotent guilt subscale (45.2 vs. 47.6, p<0.01), the empathic distress subscale (15.2 vs. 17.2, p<0.001), and especially on depressive symptoms (CES-D=13.2 vs. 21.7, p<0.001) and neuroticism (20.7 vs. 25.4, p<0.001). Buddhists scored higher on the altruism to strangers subscale, as well as on the agreeableness, conscientiousness, and openness subscales of the BFI. In the Tibetan Buddhist meditator subgroup, those whose primary goal of meditation was "other focused" (vs. self-focused) scored significantly lower on depression, empathic distress, and anxiety, and significantly higher on cognitive empathy.

Psychotic Disorder

Huang and colleagues (2011) conducted one of the first studies to examine the interaction between religion, religiosity, religious delusions, and preference for treatment in Asian patients with schizophrenia. They recruited 55 patients with schizophrenia from a university daycare clinic in Taiwan to examine these relationships. Participants were on average 37 years old, 60% were female, 13% married, and 16% had religious delusions/hallucinations. Most (82%) indicated a religious affiliation (44% Buddhism, 24% Christianity, 9% Taoism or folk religion) and 18% no religion. The questionnaire included an 8-item Religiosity Measure that assessed ritual, consequential, ideological, experiential dimensions of religious involvement (the dimensions originally conceptualized by American sociologist Charles Glock in the 1950s). Participants rated their satisfaction with psychiatric therapy and preference for psychiatric treatment, and were assessed by clinicians using the Positive and Negative Syndrome Scale (PANSS) and the Global Assessment of Functioning (GAF) Scale. Participants were divided into three groups: non-positive symptom type (NP) (n=23), positive symptom type with religious delusions/hallucinations (PR) (n=7), and positive symptom type without religious content (PN) (n=25). There was no difference in religious affiliation (present vs. absent) between the three groups. While total religiosity score (and most of the religiosity subscale scores) was significantly higher among participants with religious delusions (PR), no significant association was found between religiosity scores and psychotic symptom severity score on the PANSS. While there was no significant association between religiosity scores and satisfaction with psychiatric therapy, higher religiosity scores did correlate with a lower preference for psychiatric treatment (r=-0.54, p<0.05).

Buddhist Interventions

Rungreangkulkij and colleagues (2011) examined the effects of a Buddhist group therapy intervention on depressive symptom in 62 patients with type II diabetes seen at the Nakae Hospital diabetes clinic in Thailand. Participants were randomized to either the experimental group (n=32) or a control group (n=32). In the experimental therapy, participants were divided into four groups with eight members in each, and met for two hours weekly for six weeks (supplemented by home meditation practices). The sessions were conducted in four phases: first, rapport was established between group leaders and members; second, members were educated emphasizing the Universal Natural Laws (i.e., that "suffering comes from the members' cravings for things that are impermanent, and the members' inability to accept things that have happened"); third, emphasis was placed on practicing mindfulness consistently at home; and fourth, members perceptions, beliefs and understanding were assessed to identify causes for their symptoms and they were encouraged to practice mindfulness. The control group received "treatment as usual" by attending follow-up appointments at the diabetes clinic every month or two (i.e., this was not an active control group). The two groups were similar at baseline except that controls were more likely to be receiving current treatment with anti-depressant/anti-anxiety drugs (84.4% vs. 56.2%). Depressive symp-toms were assessed at baseline and follow-up by a nurse blind to treatment group using the Q9 (similar to the PHQ-9), which ranges in score from 0 to 24 (0-6=normal, 7-12=mild, 13-18=moderate, 19-27=severe). Treatment response was defined as a Q9 score of 0-6. Results indicated that 30 of 32 (94%) responded to treatment in the intervention group, compared to 21 of 32 (66%) in the control group (p=0.02). The effect size was 1.74 (where 0.80 or over is considered large). Given that this study involved a non-active control group, it is not possible to determine whether the reduction in anxiety was simply due to the content of the intervention or the additional social interaction and attention paid to participants in the intervention group.

Chen and colleagues (2013) conducted an intervention study in

60 Chinese nursing students (average age 20 years) at a medical University in Guangzhou, China. Participants were randomized to either mindfulness meditation training (n=30) or to a control group without meditation training (n=30). The intervention consisted of seven consecutive days of training by a senior psychological counselor proficient in mindfulness meditation. Mindfulness meditation was taught with no spiritual or religious emphasis, although incorporated traditional Chinese Buddhist cultural concepts. Those in the intervention group practiced mindfulness meditation guided by 30 minutes of standardized instruction daily throughout the seven day period. Participants self-rated themselves at baseline and immediately after the seven-day intervention using the Chinese version of the Zung Self-Rating Anxiety Scale and Zung Self-Rating Depression Scale. Results indicated a significant group by time interaction such that those receiving the active intervention decreased in anxiety compared to the control group ($p<0.001$), although there was no significant difference between groups on depressive symptoms. Again, since this study used non-active controls, the reduction in anxiety may have simply been due to the additional social attention paid to participants in the intervention group (rather than effects of mindfulness meditation).

In summary, more recent studies based on this non-systematic review show the following. In observational studies comparing the mental health of Buddhists with members of other faith traditions, the findings remain mixed (two reported better mental health in Buddhists, one reported no difference, and one found better mental health in non-Buddhists). In observational studies examining the association between religiosity and mental health in Buddhists, the majority of studies (12 of 24) found a significant positive relationship, one found a negative relationship, and the remainder reported either no relationship or mixed findings. Finally, the two clinical trials found that Buddhist interventions significantly improved mental health, but neither compared those interventions with an active/attention control group, leaving open the possibility that the benefits were due to social attention alone.

National and Cross-National Studies
Although the studies above were focused on Asian Buddhists, observational research involving large random national or inter-

national samples is rare. With only a few exceptions, most earlier and more recent studies summarized here involved non-Asian Buddhists residing in the West or non-random relatively small convenience samples of Asian Buddhists outside the West, making it difficult to generalize results to those who make up most of the world's Buddhist population. For that reason, I sought out large national datasets that included primarily Asian Buddhists to compare Buddhists with other religious groups and examine relationships between religious beliefs/practices and mental health in Buddhists. I was particularly interested in studies that included measures of religious activity that were not contaminated with indicators of mental health. Presented here, then, is information obtained from three random national and cross-national surveys comparing the mental health of Buddhists to that of members of other religious groups and to those with no religious affiliation, as well as examining relationships between religiosity and mental health in Buddhist subgroups (Koenig 2016, unpublished report) (**Table 1**).

The Spiritual Life Study of Chinese Residents (SLSCR, 2007)[1] surveyed a random sample 7,021 adults in mainland China (the country that contains almost half of all Buddhists in the world). Analyses indicated that Buddhists were equally as likely to say that they were "very happy" compared to those with no religious affiliation (33.2% vs. 33.2%), but were significantly less likely than members of other religious faiths to indicate they were very happy (33.2% vs. 42.3%, p<0.05). Other religious affiliations in this sample were primarily of Christians (73%), Muslims (12%), and Taoists (10%). Given that many Chinese Buddhists are not active in their religious faith, the analysis was repeated among those who were at least "somewhat religious." The findings were similar (33.0% of Buddhists indicated they were very happy vs. 42.5% of those

---

[1] *Spiritual Life Study of Chinese Residents 2007* surveyed a random sample of 7,021 Chinese citizens ages 16-75 in 2007. Sampling involved a multi-stage method to select metropolitan cities, towns and administrative villages. The survey was administered in 56 locales throughout China, including 3 cities (Beijing, Shanghai, Chongqing) and 6 province capital cities (Guangzhou, Nanjing, Wuhan, Hefei, Xi'an and Chengdu). In addition, 11 regional level cities, 16 small towns, and 20 villages were sampled. Kish method used to select one person per household for face-to-face in-home interviews. Data were downloaded from the Association of Religion Data Archives, www.TheARDA.com, and collected by Dr. Anna Sun and research team, funded by the John Templeton Foundation (accessed 11/7/16).

affiliated with other religious groups). When asked to list the top three reasons for why they felt happy, Buddhists were less likely than members of other religious groups to list "my religious life" among those reasons. Importance of religious belief in life, however, was not related to happiness in either Buddhists (r=0.02, p=0.43, n=1111) or those affiliated with other religious groups (r=-0.03, p=0.63, n=239). This finding no cross-sectional relationship between religiosity and mental health is common in countries such as China where religion is in disfavor (64.7% of this sample had no religious affiliation). Importance of religion is often an "indicator" of mental stress in such countries, where the threshold for turning to religion is much higher and only those who are suffering significant distress do so (Hvidt et al., 2017).

In the International Social Survey Program (ISSP, 2008),[1] a cross-national survey involving a random sample of over 59,000 adults from 40 countries, Buddhists (most of who were from Taiwan, Japan, and South Korea) were again significantly less likely than those with other religious affiliations to indicate they were very happy (19.2% vs. 26.7, p<0.0001). In that study, other religious faiths were again primarily Christian (86%) and Muslim (5%). As in the SLSCR study, the difference was similar among those who indicated they were at least somewhat religious. However, Buddhists were similar to members of other faith traditions in saying that religion helps people "find inner peace and happiness" (32.1% vs. 35.4%), although among those who were at least somewhat religious, Buddhists were less likely to say so (39.3% vs. 44.7%, p<0.05). Buddhists were also significantly less likely to say that religion helps people "gain comfort

---

[1] *International Social Survey Program 2008* surveyed a random sample of 59,063 citizens ages 15 to 90 from 40 countries (Australia, Austria, Belgium - Flanders, Chile, Croatia, Cyprus, Czech Republic, Denmark, Dominican Republic, Finland, France, Germany, Great Britain, Hungary, Ireland, Israel, Italy, Japan, Latvia, Mexico, Netherlands, New Zealand, Northern Ireland, Norway, Philippines, Poland, Portugal, Russia, Slovakia, Slovenia, Spain, South Korea, South Africa, Sweden, Switzerland, Taiwan, Turkey, Ukraine, Uruguay, the United States of America, Venezuela, Taiwan, Japan, and South Korea). Most Buddhists came from Japan (32.4%), Taiwan (31.9%), South Korea (29.3%). Interviews were conducted face-to-face, by telephone, and through self-completed postal questionnaires; collected by Dr. Max Haller and his team at the Institut für Soziologie, Universität Graz, Austria (accessed 11/7/16). The data were downloaded from Association of Religion Data Archives, www.TheARDA.com.

in times of trouble or sorrow" compared with non-Buddhists (27.1% vs. 39.4%, p<0.0001), with similar results among those who indicated they were at least somewhat religious. Among Buddhists overall, self-rated religiosity was weakly but positively related to happiness (r=0.07, p=0.02, n=1194).

In the World Values Survey (WVS, 2005-2006),[1] a random cross-national survey of over 83,000 adults from 80 countries, however, the results were different. In that study, Buddhists (primarily from Thailand, China, Japan, South Korea, Taiwan, and Hong Kong) were significantly *more likely* to report that they were "very happy" compared to members of other religious groups (31.5% vs. 28.2%,

---

[1] *World Values Survey 2005-2006* surveyed a random national sample of 83,879 adults ages 18 to 85 from more than 80 countries (approximately 1000 per country using full probability sampling). Of the 80 countries, one country has Buddhists primarily from the Theravada branch of Buddhism (Thailand [n=1,480]) and the remaining Southeast Asian countries have Buddhists primarily from the Mahayana branch (China [n=71], Japan [n=341], S Korea [n=300], Taiwan [n=227], Hong Kong [n=160]). The mode of data collection for WVS survey was face-to-face interviewing. This project was carried out by an international network of social scientists, with local funding for each survey. The data were downloaded from the World Values Survey (WORLD VALUES SURVEY Wave 5 2005-2008 OFFICIAL AGGREGATE v.20140429. World Values Survey Association [www.worldvaluessurvey.org].
Aggregate File Producer: Asep/JDS, Madrid SPAIN) retrieved from
http://www.worldvaluessurvey.org/WVSDocumentationWV5.jsp (accessed 11-7-16)

Table 1. All Buddhists and "religious" Buddhists compared with other religious groups and the non-affiliated on happiness and satisfaction with life

	Buddhists % (N)/Mean (SD)	Non-Buddhists % (N)/Mean (SD)	No Affiliation % (N)/Mean (SD)
Chinese Spirituality Study 2007	100.0 (1168)	100.0 (246)	100.0 (5,482)
Do you feel happy about your life overall?			
Very happy	33.2 (387) *[1]	42.3 (104)	33.2 (1,818) *[2]
Somewhat happy	49.0 (571)	41.9 (103)	47.0 (2,574)
Less than somewhat happy	17.8 (207)	15.9 (39)	19.8 (2,085)
Among those who are at least "somewhat R":			
Very happy	33.0 (273) *	42.5 (77)	31.1 (391) *
Somewhat happy	49.3 (408)	40.9 (74)	48.6 (612)
Less than somewhat happy	17.7 (146)	16.6 (30)	20.3 (256)
Main reasons why feel happy (top 3)			
First reason is R	0.2 (2) ^{ns}	0.5 (1)	0.1 (2) ^{ns}
Second reason is R	2.0 (18) *	4.5 (9)	0.0 (1) ****
Third reason is R	5.6 (41) ***	13.4 (20)	0.2 (6) ****
International Social Survey Program 2008	100.0 (1,224)	100.0 (45,438)	100.0 (12,557)
How happy are you? (very happy)	19.2 (232) ****	26.7 (11,886)	22.2 (2,714) ****
Among those who are at least "somewhat R":			
Very happy	20.9 (171) ****	28.3 (8,071)	28.4 (375) **
R helps people find inner peace/happiness			
Strongly agree	32.1 (375) ^{ns}	35.4 (15,112)	12.1 (1,365) ****
Agree	51.4 (601)	48.3 (20,601)	44.9 (5,044)
Do not strongly agree nor agree	16.6 (194)	16.3 (6,956)	43.0 (4,834)
Among those who are at least "somewhat R":			
Strongly agree	39.3 (318) *	44.7 (12,270)	24.9 (318) ****
Agree	51.6 (418)	46.4 (12,754)	52.4 (669)
Do not strongly agree nor agree	9.1 (74)	8.9 (2,448)	22.7 (290)
R helps people find comfort during sorrow/trauma			
Strongly agree	27.1 (314) ****	39.4 (16,876)	17.9 (2,039) ****
Agree	55.6 (644)	47.7 (20,427)	52.0 (5,933)
Do not strongly agree nor agree	17.3 (201)	12.9 (5,521)	30.2 (3,447)
Among those who are at least "somewhat R":			
Strongly agree	32.1 (258) ****	47.8 (13,117)	33.6 (432) *
Agree	56.7 (455)	44.0 (12,093)	55.1 (707)
Do not strongly agree nor agree	11.2 (90)	8.2 (2,250)	11.3 (145)

Table 1 (continued). All Buddhists and "religious" Buddhists compared with other religious groups and the non-affiliated on happiness and satisfaction with life

	Buddhists % (N)/Mean (SD)	Non-Buddhists % (N)/Mean (SD)	No Affiliation % (N)/Mean (SD)
World Values Survey 2005-2006	100.0 (3,266)	100.0 (64,737)	100.0 (14,631)
Taking all things together, how happy?			
Very happy	31.5 (1,022) ****[1]	28.2 (18,416)	26.9 (3,888)****[2]
Those for whom R is very or rather important:			
Taking all things together, how happy?			
Very happy	35.1 (846) ****	28.0 (14,214)	30.5 (860) ****
Satisfied with life as a whole			
(1=not, 10=very)	6.99 (1.92) **** (n=3,251)	6.65 (2.40) (n=65,250)	6.94 (2.10) **** (n=14,507)
Those for whom R is very or rather important:			
Satisfied with life as a whole			
(1=not, 10=very)	7.11 (1.88) **** (n=2,411)	6.49 (2.45) (n=50,570)	6.89 (2.21) **** (n=2,814)

R=religion or religious
[ns]=not significant (p≥0.05); *p<0.05; **p<0.01; ***p<0.001; ****p<0.0001, where Mantel-Haenszel χ^2 used to compare Buddhists and other religious groups where outcome ordinal; χ^2 for categorical outcomes; Student t-test for comparison of continuous outcomes between two groups; analysis of variance for comparison of continuous outcomes between 3 groups
[1]applies to difference between Buddhists and non-Buddhists
[2]differences between all 3 groups

p<0.0001), with similar (if not stronger) results among those indicating religion was important in their lives. Members of other religious groups were again primarily Christian (61.4%) and Muslim (23.1%). This finding was primarily present among Buddhist from Thailand (a highly religious and largely Buddhist country). When Thai Buddhists were removed from the sample, the findings completely reversed (23.7% of non-Thai Buddhists indicated they were very happy, compared to 28.2% of members of other religious faiths, p<0.0001). When asked how satisfied they were with their lives as a whole (on a scale from 1=completely dissatisfied to 10=completely satisfied), Buddhists in the overall sample rated themselves significantly higher on satisfaction than members of other religious groups (7.11 vs. 6.49, p<0.0001). This finding, though, was also present when Thai Buddhists were removed from the sample (6.80 vs. 6.64, p<0.005).

As noted in the last chapter, Buddhists overall in the WVS were less likely than members of other religious groups to say that religion was "very important" to them (38.0% vs. 58.0%, p<0.0001) (see Table 3 in chapter 4). However, self-rated importance of religion among Buddhists in the WVS was positively related to both greater happiness in life (r=0.21, p<0.0001, n=3193) and to greater life satisfaction (r=0.14, p<0.0001, n=3194).

Conclusions

The studies above compare the mental health of Buddhists and non-Buddhists, examine the relationship between religiosity and mental health in Buddhists, and review Buddhist interventions for improving mental health. With regard to Buddhists vs. non-Buddhists, our systematic review of five studies published *prior to 2010* found that three favored Buddhists over non-Buddhists, one found no difference, and one reported worse mental health; among studies *since 2010*, two found better mental health in Buddhists, one found no difference, and one reported worse mental health. In three large random national and cross-national studies, one found better mental health in Buddhists (but only Buddhists in Thailand) and the other two reported worse mental health in Buddhists compared to non-Buddhists. Thus, the findings are mixed, making conclusions difficult to make. While there is every reason because of core Buddhist beliefs (see chapter 5) to expect Buddhists to have better mental health than non-Buddhists, then, this is not always so. With regard to the relationship between religiosity and mental health in Buddhists, nearly half of the research (46% or 18 of 39 studies) reported that greater religiosity among Buddhists is associated with better mental health in (4 of 12 earlier studies; 12 of 24 recent studies; 2 of 3 large cross-national random samples); 4 studies (10%) reported worse mental health; and the remainder (44%) reported no association or mixed findings. Finally, all six intervention studies (100%) show that treatments based on Buddhist beliefs/ practices improve mental health (although adequacy of control groups was an issue). In conclusion, these findings suggest that when Buddhists commit to and follow the core Buddhist principles outlined in the Eightfold Path that they usually experience good mental health.

CHAPTER 8

CLINICAL APPLICATIONS

What, then, does the mental health professional, pastoral counselor or Buddhist clergy do with this information? I begin with a case vignette to illustrate a situation that helping professionals may find themselves in when seeking to help Buddhist clients.

Case Vignette

Mr. James Wong has been seeing a mental health counselor for several months now. James has experienced several traumatic losses over the past year, including the death of his son in a car accident, decreased income from a failing business, and marital problems at home. Always an anxious person, these changes have caused him to feel more anxious, and he is now overwhelmed and becoming less and less able to function. While antidepressants from his psychiatrist have helped, symptoms remain. As part of the intake history, his counselor asked James if he had any religious or spiritual beliefs that are important to him. James had said that he was raised in a Buddhist family and that he and his wife were active on and off in their temple, but doesn't follow Buddhist practices as he should. Seeking to identify nonpharmacological resources that might help relieve his distress, the counselor asked James if his Buddhist beliefs played a role in his life now. James acknowledges that his religious faith is important to him and his family. His counselor asked him to explain. James described how his Buddhist beliefs have provided him comfort after the death of his son. When the counselor asks if James had ever engaged in any form of meditation, he said he had not. The counselor then suggested he read *The Miracle of Mindfulness* (Hanh, 1999) and consider practicing daily meditation, and also to read *What the Buddha Taught* (Rahula, 1974) to help him further understand the religious roots of mindfulness as originally practiced within the context of the Eightfold Path.

The suggestions I make in this chapter are based on knowledge about Buddhist beliefs and practices discussed earlier, evidence from systematic research, clinical experience with faith-based interventions, and simply common sense.

1. Take a Spiritual History

When encountering Buddhist clients, ask if Buddhist beliefs and practices are important to them either now or in the past (including during their youth). If not important at all, then the subject may be dropped. If even somewhat important, take a detailed spiritual history to learn about those beliefs and practices. Taking the time to ask about their religious beliefs and practices is by itself an intervention that will underscore their importance and boost the effectiveness of those beliefs as a resource for coping.

The spiritual history above should always be taken on initial evaluation, or soon afterwards. The purpose of the spiritual history is to identify the specific Buddhist beliefs of the client, the importance of those beliefs to the person, and the extent to which beliefs and practices are adhered to. Finally, both good and bad experiences with Buddhism across the client's lifetime should be explored. This information will be valuable in deciding on the treatment approach and in providing treatment that meets the minimum standard of showing respect for clients' personal beliefs and values (as required by most credentialing organizations in the U.S.). Mental health professionals should assume nothing in this regard, but rather have each client educate them about (a) what role their Buddhist beliefs/practices play in life, (b) how these beliefs help them to cope with their illness or associated life stressors, (c) if a non-traditional healer or faith healer has been sought previously for treatment (and the results), and (d) how Buddhist beliefs or practices may be initiating, worsening or maintaining the illness. In particular, it is important to understand what the client feels is the underlying cause of the illness, especially the role that "bad karma" may be playing.

Taking a spiritual history is the most important recommendation that I can make when treating Buddhist patients. If the therapist is uncomfortable asking about religious issues (i.e., taking a spiritual history) then such resistance must be overcome with training and practice.

2. Asks about the Family/Broader Community

Buddhist clients will each come out of a particular family and community of friends and support persons. Unlike Westerners who treasure their independence and self-sufficiency, Buddhists (like Hindus) are often heavily dependent on relationships within the family and the community (as part of South Asian culture). Therefore, religious beliefs and religiosity of the client's family of origin, and the religious beliefs and religiosity of the client's support system need to be inquired about as well. This will give the clinician a sense of whether changes made during therapy will be supported (or opposed) after the client leaves the therapist's office. Although client confidentiality should be maintained at all times, and most clinical encounters will involve only the client and the treating professional, there will be times when the therapist will need to ask permission from the patient to include the family during the assessment and the treatment.

3. Be Supportive

Be respectful and supportive of the Buddhist client's religious beliefs/practices that he or she finds helpful (or might find helpful in the future) as a way of coping with emotional issues. However, always do so from the client's perspective. If the client is receptive and open to healthy religious practices, and these beliefs/practices are not clearly pathological, then they may be encouraged. If the client shows any resistance, don't push; however, it may be informative to gently explore where the resistance to religious beliefs/practices is coming from in a future session. Never give clients the impression that they are not religious enough, since they probably get plenty of that from family members or those in their religious community. Whether you are a psychiatrist prescribing biological therapies or a therapist providing counseling, the mental health professional should be viewed by the client as neutral, interested in, open to and supportive of the client's Buddhist faith tradition, but always on the client's side and never judgmental. This advice also applies to Buddhist clergy who may be counseling members of their temple or religious community.

4. Provide a Safe Place
Provide an open and safe place where clients can talk freely about their religion, good or bad, without judgment. Maintain a respectful, interested, and receptive attitude at all times with regard to the client's Buddhist beliefs and practices (whether the person is currently active in their faith tradition or not, whether he or she speaks well of their tradition or not).

5. Utilize Buddhist Resources
If the client is religious and the therapist plans to provide secular psychotherapy, then that therapy should (as noted above) be supportive and respectful of the client's Buddhist beliefs. There may also be times during secular psychotherapy when the client's religious beliefs can be utilized to support changes in attitude and behavior. Knowing about those religious beliefs/practices (as described in earlier chapters) will be helpful, as will a detailed spiritual history to identify ones that are particularly important to the Buddhist client. Consultation with knowledgeable experts in Buddhism may be needed as well, particularly if beliefs are to be challenged (see below).

When encountering Buddhist patients who are open to learning more about Buddhist beliefs, suggest that they read something that describes the core beliefs of their particular branch of Buddhism. Many of these core beliefs directly address issues related to emotional and mental suffering. Buddhists from all traditions will find common ground in the Dhammapada (the translation by Carter and Palihawadana is simple and easy to read for Buddhists fluent in

English). Suggest they read 2-3 verses each morning, and then spend 15-20 minutes thinking about their meaning and how they might be applied in the day ahead and the problems currently being faced. Encourage them to spend no more than 30 minutes total each day on this activity. During the next visit, ask about what they learned.

6. **Consider a Religiously-Integrated Therapy**

If clients prefer this approach and therapists are willing and qualified, religiously-integrated cognitive behavioral therapy (CBT) from a Buddhist perspective should be considered for those with emotional disorders. There are resources that may help the therapist or Buddhist clergy in this regard. This includes a Buddhist CBT manual, along with therapist and patient workbooks, and an introductory video, that can be accessed at the Center for Spirituality, Theology and Health website, all without charge (CSTH, 2014). Religiously-integrated CBT, including that from a Buddhist perspective, is an evidence-based treatment that has documented effectiveness in the treatment for depression, especially in highly religious patients (Koenig et al., 2015).

Therapists and pastoral counselors should also consider other evidence-based Buddhist treatments such as Vipassana meditation (Emavardhana and Tori, 1997), 3-S Therapy (Margolin et al, 2006), Buddhist counseling (Rungreangkulkij & Wongakee, 2008), Buddhist group therapy (Rungreangkulkij et al, 2011), mindfulness-based treatments (Chen et al, 2013), and even recommend going on a Buddhist retreat (Tori, 1999) (see Buddhist Interventions in Chapters 6 and 7).

7. **Less Formal Approaches to Integration**

A less formal approach to integrating Buddhist beliefs into therapy might involve asking Buddhist patients what they know about the Four Noble Truths and the Eightfold Path. Next, ask them if they would be open to discussing each of the eight steps with you. Go over only one step in each session, and if they are open, suggest they think about and practice the step during the time before the next session (and then report on their experiences). Be alert for any discomfort or resistance, and gently explore this with them. Never be coercive, and if the therapist senses persistent discomfort with this method, then stop and proceed with more standard secular counseling.

Another approach is to suggest that Buddhist patients spend 15-20 minutes each day in mindfulness meditation (*samma sati*) or concentration meditation (*samma samadhi*), but only after they have read something that explains how these practices are integrated within the Eightfold Path. Indicate that when mindfulness is practiced within such a religious context, that the benefits are likely to be much greater than if the only goal is pain relief or distraction (although not yet fully proven through systematic research, such a conclusion is reasonable based on what is known so far).

8. **Accommodate the Environment**

In office or hospital settings, every effort should be made to accommodate the environment to make it easier for Buddhist patients to practice their religion (or indicate evidence that the therapist is sensitive and supportive). This may include placing a copy of *The Dhammapada* (Carter & Palihawadana, 2000) or *The Miracle of Mindfulness* (Hanh, 1999) on a table in the waiting room. In the hospital, this may include accommodating the chapel so that Buddhist patients feel comfortable worshiping in this setting.

9. **Challenge/Re-Educate**

If the client's Buddhist beliefs or practices are contributing to their psychopathology, and this is confirmed following consultation with an expert from the client's local Buddhist congregation (after the client provides consent), then the following approach is suggested. First and foremost, the mental health professional should inquire further about the role that particular religious beliefs are playing in supporting psychopathology. The therapist should listen respectfully, gathering as much information as possible about the natural history of how religion became intertwined with the emotional problem. This must be done in an open and receptive manner and without confrontation (at least initially during this information gathering stage). There will come a time, once the therapeutic relationship is firmly established and the client feels safe and accepted, when gradual, gentle, and persistent "Socratic questioning" may help to guide the client towards a "healthier" use of their Buddhist beliefs/practices. I emphasize *gradual, gentle, and persistent questioning* by an informed therapist within an atmosphere that is safe and comfortable. Arguments over religious beliefs will almost always be unsuccessful and will adversely affect the therapeutic alliance.

10. **Proceed Cautiously and Gently**

As noted above, always proceed cautiously and gently when exploring religious beliefs and practices with Buddhist clients, especially as noted above when challenging Buddhist beliefs, but also when making suggests regarding readings or practices at home (and when processing the resulting experiences with clients). Don't be reluctant to explore with the client any discomfort or resistances that emerge (either within the therapist or the client), but be sure this is done with the utmost of sensitivity. All interventions must be client-centered, not therapist-centered. As noted earlier, allowing Buddhist clients to explore their own beliefs and practices in a safe and supportive atmosphere at their own pace may be more important than any advice given by the therapist. Listening carefully and creating a safe space to explore those beliefs is the therapist's primary goal.

11. **Consult or Refer**

If addressing religion or integrating it into the treatment seems indicated in a Buddhist client, and the therapist lacks the desire or experience to do so, consideration should be given to consultation with, co-therapy with, or referral to a Buddhist chaplain[1] or pastoral counselor.[2] If clergy trained to provide counseling from a Buddhist perspective are not available, then the therapist should consider obtaining additional training in this regard (see CSTH, 2014).

12. **Non-Religious Buddhists**

If the client was raised in a Buddhist family but is not actively religious, then the mental health professional should proceed with secular psychotherapy that is respectful of the client's personal and

---

[1] Directory of Buddhist Chaplains. *Buddhist Chaplains.org: Community, Resources, Momentum.* See http://buddhistchaplains.org/cmsms/index.php?page=our-directory

[2] New York Zen Center for Contemplative Care. See http://zencare.org/; Won Institute. See https://www.woninstitute.edu/academics/certificate-in-buddhist-pastoral-care/; or American Association of Pastoral Counselors. See http://aapc.org/Default.aspx?ssid=74&NavPTypeId=1708 (place Buddhist for denomination)

cultural beliefs. Aggressive attempts to reconnect the person to his/her Buddhist faith tradition should be avoided. If the client was once religious and has now become socially isolated or is despairing for lack of meaning in life, the therapist might gently ask if the client has considered re-establishing connections with a local faith community. The therapist may help the client weigh the pluses and minuses of such re-involvement, but again always from the client's perspective and following the client's lead.

Conclusions

In this chapter I have made a number of suggestions on how to apply knowledge about Buddhist beliefs/practices and information from systematic research to the care of Buddhist clients with emotional or mental health problems. The most important recommendations stressed here are to take a detailed spiritual history, be supportive and respectful of the person's Buddhist beliefs, utilize those beliefs/ practices (when not pathological) in the treatment, and always utilize a client-centered approach that is sensitive and gentle. If re-education or confrontation is needed to address religious beliefs or practices that are contributing to the client's illness, then the therapist should proceed cautiously and usually only after guidance has been sought from experts in the Buddhist tradition.

CHAPTER 9

FINAL CONCLUSIONS

As in other world religions, there are widespread differences in Buddhist belief and practice, depending on the particular part of the world in which the person lives (or if living in a Western country, where they or their family immigrated from). Knowing something about Buddhist beliefs and practices in Theravada, Mahayana, and Vajrayana traditions (as reviewed in this book) will be helpful when counseling Buddhist clients. Systematic research on Buddhism and mental health as reviewed in Chapters 6 and 7 may help to inform clinicians about evidence-based approaches for treating Buddhist clients. Although there is great need for more systematic research, a number of tentative conclusions can be made about the relationship between Buddhism and mental health.

Research suggests that Buddhists who are active in their faith tradition are often happier, more satisfied with life, and cope better with stress (even the horrific stress encountered with torture). This is not true for all Buddhists, however, particularly those who are only marginally religious or living in areas of the world where Buddhist beliefs are not supported or encouraged (as has been the case in China until just recently). Certain Buddhist practices, such as mindfulness and other forms of meditation may be helpful to Buddhist patients, particularly if practiced within the context of the Eightfold Path and integrated with core Buddhist teachings.

Buddhist clients may also be receptive to religiously-integrated forms for counseling described here, and I have provided suggestions and resources in this regard. Regardless of whether Buddhist beliefs and practices are integrated into therapy or not, the mental health professional should always take a detailed spiritual history so that mental health care is client-centered and provided in a way that is sensitive to and supportive of the Buddhist client's personal beliefs and values.

REFERENCES

Ambedkar BR (1957). Conversion of Anathapindika (section 5, part III, book 2). In *The Buddha and His Dhamma*. Mumbai, India: Siddhartha College Publications. Retrieved from http://www.columbia.edu/itc/mealac/pritchett/00ambedkar/ambedkar_buddha/02_3.html (accessed 10/29/16).

Anonymous (date unknown). Abstract: The Lotus Sutra. The Salvation Religions, 200 BCE to 900 CE. *Oxford First Source*. Retrieved from http://www.oxfordfirstsource.com/view/10.1093/acref/978019939 9680.013.0189/acref-9780199399680-e-189?result=72&rskey=CZU3e0&mediaType=Article (accessed on 10/28/16)

ARDA (2016). International, national profiles. *Association of Religion Data Archives*. Retrieved from http://www.thearda.com/internationalData/ (accessed on11/6/16).

Assanangkornchai, S., Conigrave, K. M., Saunders, J. B. (2002). Religious beliefs and practice, and alcohol use in Thai men. *Alcohol & Alcoholism, 37*(2), 193-197.

Assanangkornchai, S., Sam-Angsri, N., Rerngpongpan, S., & Lertnakorn, A. (2010). Patterns of alcohol consumption in the Thai population: results of the National Household Survey of 2007. *Alcohol and Alcoholism, 45*(3), 278-285.

Babbitt EC (2009). *Jataka Tales*. Radford, VA: Wilder Publications

Bodhi, B. (2005). *In the Buddha's Words: An Anthology of Discourses from the Pali Canon* (The Teachings of the Buddha). Somerville, MA: Wisdom Publications

Borg M, Kornfield J (1999). *Jesus and Buddha: The Parallel Sayings*. Berkeley, CA: Ulysses Press

Boyd, K. A., & Chung, H. (2012). Opinions toward suicide: Cross-national evaluation of cultural and religious effects on individuals. *Social Science Research*, *41*(6), 1565-1580.

Carter JR, Palihawadana M (2000). *The Dhammapada: The Sayings of the Buddha* (Oxford World's Classics). Oxford, UK: Oxford University Press

Chamratrithirong A, Miller BA, Byrnes HF, Rhucharoenpornpanich O, Cupp PK, Rosati MJ, Fongkaew W, Atwood KA, Chookhare W (2010). Spirituality within the family and the prevention of health risk behavior among adolescents in Bangkok, Thailand. *Social Sciences and Medicine* 71(10):1855-1863

Chen, Y., Yang, X., Wang, L., & Zhang, X. (2013). A randomized controlled trial of the effects of brief mindfulness meditation on anxiety symptoms and systolic blood pressure in Chinese nursing students. *Nurse Education Today*, *33*(10), 1166-1172.

Chiesa, A., & Serretti, A. (2009). Mindfulness-based stress reduction for stress management in healthy people: a review and meta-analysis. *Journal of Alternative and Complementary Medicine*, *15*(5), 593-600.

Clarke, T. C., Black, L. I., Stussman, B. J., Barnes, P. M., & Nahin, R. L. (2015). Trends in the use of complementary health approaches among adults: United States, 2002–2012. *National Health Statistics Reports*, 79:1-15

Conze E, transator (1959). *Buddhist Scriptures*. London: Penguin

Cook, D., & Hayes, S. C. (2010). Acceptance-based coping and the psychological adjustment of Asian and Caucasian Americans. *International Journal of Behavioral Consultation and Therapy*, *6*(3), 186-197.

Cooke J (2010). *Meditation in Modern Buddhism: Renunciation and Change in Thai Monastic Life*. Cambridge, UK: Cambridge University Press, p 2

CSTH (2014). *Religious Cognitive Behavioral Therapy: Buddhist Version.* Durham, North Carolina: Duke University Center for Spirituality, Theology and Health. Retrieved from: http://www.spiritualityandhealth.duke.edu/index.php/religious-cbt-study/therapy-manuals (accessed on 12/9/16).

De Jong, JW (1993). The beginnings of Buddhism. *The Eastern Buddhist N.S.* 26 (2):11-30

De La Vallée Poussin, L. (1922). Suicide (Buddhist). In Hastings J (ed), XII *Encyclopaedia of Religion and Ethics* 24. Edinburgh: T. and T. Clark, p 25

Dhammayut Order (2013). *A Chanting Guide: Pali Passages with English Translations.* Valley Center, CA: Metta Forest Monastery, p 42

Emavardhana, T., & Tori, C. D. (1997). Changes in self-concept, ego defense mechanisms, and religiosity following seven-day Vipassana meditation retreats. *Journal for the Scientific Study of Religion* 36(2):194-206.

Encyclopedia Britannica (2004). Buddhism. *Encyclopedia Britannica Premium Service.* Retrieved from https://www.britannica.com/topic/Buddhism (accessed on 10/28/16)

Falb, M. D., & Pargament, K. I. (2013). Buddhist coping predicts psychological outcomes among end-of-life caregivers. *Psychology of Religion and Spirituality*, 5(4), 252-262.

Falk, M. L. (2010). Recovery and Buddhist practices in the aftermath of the Tsunami in Southern Thailand. *Religion*, 40(2), 96-103.

Fazel, M. K., & Young, D. M. (1988). Life quality of Tibetans and Hindus: A function of religion. *Journal for the Scientific Study of Religion*, 229-242.

Gethin, R (1998). *Foundations of Buddhism.* NY, NY: Oxford University Press

Grossman, P., Niemann, L., Schmidt, S., & Walach, H. (2004). Mindfulness-based stress reduction and health benefits: A meta-analysis. *Journal of Psychosomatic Research, 57*(1), 35-43.

Groves, P., & Farmer, R. (1994). Buddhism and addictions. *Addiction Research, 2*(2), 183-194.

Hanh TN (1999a). *The Heart of the Buddha's Teaching.* New York, NY: Broadway Books (hardcover edition originally published in 1998 by Parallax Press)

Hanh TN (1999b). *The Miracle of Mindfulness.* Boston, MA: Beacon Press

Hollifield, M., Hewage, C., Gunawardena, C. N., Kodituwakku, P., Bopagoda, K., Weerarathnege, K., et al. (2008). Symptoms and coping in Sri Lanka 20-21 months after the 2004 tsunami. *British Journal of Psychiatry, 192*(1), 39-44.

Holtz, T. H. (1998). Refugee trauma versus torture trauma: a retrospective controlled cohort study of Tibetan refugees. *Journal of Nervous and Mental Disease, 186*(1), 24-34.

Huang, C. L. C., Shang, C. Y., Shieh, M. S., Lin, H. N., & Su, J. C. J. (2011). The interactions between religion, religiosity, religious delusion/hallucination, and treatment-seeking behavior among schizophrenic patients in Taiwan. *Psychiatry Research* 187(3), 347-353.

Hui, V. K. Y., & Coleman, P. G. (2012). Do reincarnation beliefs protect older adult Chinese Buddhists against personal death anxiety? *Death Studies, 36*(10), 949-958.

Hvidt NC, Hvidtjørn D, Christensen K, Nielsen JB, Søndergaard J (2017). Faith moves mountains-mountains move faith: Two opposite epidemiological forces in research on religion and health. *Journal of Religion and Health* 56(1): 294–304

Hyodo, I., Amano, N., Eguchi, K., Narabayashi, M., Imanishi, J., Hirai, M., ... & Takashima, S. (2005). Nationwide survey on complementary and alternative medicine in cancer patients in Japan. *Journal of Clinical Oncology, 23*(12), 2645-2654.

Insight Meditation Society (2017). *Glossary of Buddhist Terms.* Retrieved from https://www.dharma.org/resources/glossary (accessed on 5/24/17)

ISSP (2008). *International Social Survey Program*, 2008. Dataset downloaded from the Association of Religion Data Archives, www.TheARDA.com, and were collected by Dr. Max Haller and his team at the Institut für Soziologie, Universität Graz, Austria (accessed on 11/7/16).

Jang, J. E., Kim, S. W., Kim, S. Y., Kim, J. M., Park, M. H., Yoon, J. H., Shin HY, Kang HJ, Bae KY, Shin IS, Yoon, J. S. (2013). Religiosity, depression, and quality of life in Korean patients with breast cancer: a 1-year prospective longitudinal study. *Psycho-Oncology, 22*(4), 922-929.

Jayaram V (2015). *The Buddha on God.* Retrieved from http://www.hinduwebsite.com/buddhism/buddhaongod.asp (accessed on 10/28/16)

Johnson WJ (1994). *The Bhagavad Gita* (reissued in 2008 as part of Oxford World Classics series). NY, NY: Oxford University Press

Kalupahana DJ (1975). *Causality: The Central Philosophy of Buddhism.* Honolulu, HI: University Press of Hawaii, p 83

Keller, A., Lhewa, D., Rosenfeld, B., Sachs, E., Aladjem, A., Cohen, I., et al. (2006). Traumatic experiences and psychological distress in an urban refugee population seeking treatment services. *Journal of Nervous and Mental Disease, 194*(3), 188-194.

Keown, D. (1996). Buddhism and suicide: The case of Channa. *Journal of Buddhist Ethics 3*(8): 8-31

Khumsaen, N., Aoup-por, W., & Thammachak, P. (2012). Factors influencing quality of life among people living with HIV (PLWH) in Suphanburi Province, Thailand. *Journal of the Association of Nurses in AIDS Care, 23*(1), 63-72.

Kim, A. E. (2003). Religious influences on personal and societal well-being. *Social Indicators Research, 62-63*(1-3), 149-170.

Kim, H. A., & Seo, Y. I. (2003). Use of complementary and alternative medicine by arthritis patients in a university hospital clinic serving rheumatology patients in Korea. *Rheumatology International, 23*(6), 277-281.

Knapp S (2016). God is both personal (Bhagavan) and impersonal (Brahman). http://www.stephen-knapp.com/god_is_both_%20personal_(Bhagavan)_and_impersonal_(Brahman).htm (accessed 8/12/16)

Koenig HG (2016). Unpublished report. Based on analysis of data downloaded from the ARDA Archive that contains the 2007 Spiritual Life Study of Chinese Residents, the 2008 International Social Survey Program, and the 2005-2006 World Values Survey datasets. Retrieved from: http://www.thearda.com/archive/browse.asp (last accessed 12/9/16).

Koenig HG, King DE, Carson VB (2012). *Handbook of Religion and Health*, 2nd ed. New York, NY: Oxford University Press

Koenig HG, McCullough ME, Larson DB (2001). *Handbook of Religion and Health*, 1st ed. NY, NY: Oxford University Press

Koenig HG, Pearce MJ, Nelson B, Shaw SF, Robins CJ, Daher N, Cohen HJ, Berk LS, Bellinger D, Pargament KI, Rosmarin DH, Vasegh S, Kristeller J, Juthani N, Nies D, King MB (2015). Religious vs. conventional cognitive-behavioral therapy for major depression in persons with chronic medical illness. *Journal of Nervous and Mental Disease* 203(4):243-251

Koenig, H. G. (2008). Concerns about measuring "spirituality" in research. *Journal of Nervous & Mental Disease, 196*(5), 349-355

Krause, N., Ingersoll-Dayton, B., Liang, J., & Sugisawa, H. (1999). Religion, social support, and health among the Japanese elderly. *Journal of Health and Social Behavior*, 40(4): 405-421.

Kuijpers, H. J. H., Van der Heijden, F. M. M. A., Tuinier, S., & Verhoeven, W. M. A. (2007). Meditation-induced psychosis. *Psychopathology, 40*(6), 461-464.

Kuyken, W., Warren, F. C., Taylor, R. S., Whalley, B., Crane, C., Bondolfi, G., Hayes R, Huijbers M, Ma H, Schweizer S, Segal Z, Speckens A, Teasdale JD, Van Heeringen K, Williams M, Byford S, Byng R, Dalgleish T. (2016). Efficacy of mindfulness-based cognitive therapy in prevention of depressive relapse: An individual patient data meta-analysis from randomized trials. *JAMA Psychiatry, 73*(6), 565-574.

Leighton, TD (1998). *Bodhisattva Archetypes: Classic Buddhist Guides to Awakening and Their Modern Expression.* New York, NY: Penguin Arkana, pp. 158–205.

Levy, B. R., Slade, M. D., & Ranasinghe, P. (2009). Causal thinking after a tsunami wave: Karma beliefs, pessimistic explanatory style and health among Sri Lankan survivors. *Journal of Religion and Health, 48*(1), 38-45.

Lewis R (2012). Buddhism and meditation: Why most Buddhists in the world don't meditate. *Huffington Post.* Retrieved from: http://www.huffingtonpost.com/lewis-richmond/most-buddhists-dont-medit_b_1461821.html (last accessed 10/28/16)

Li, H., Xu, L., Chi, I. (2016). Factors related to Chinese older adults' suicidal thoughts and attempts. *Aging & Mental Health* 20(7):752-761.

Li, X., & Phillips, M. R. (2015). The acceptability of suicide among rural residents, urban residents, and college students from three locations in China. *Crisis* 31(4):183-193

Lim, M. K., Sadarangani, P., Chan, H. L., & Heng, J. Y. (2005). Complementary and alternative medicine use in multiracial Singapore. *Complementary Therapies in Medicine, 13*(1), 16-24.

Limlomwongse, N., & Liabsuetrakul, T. (2006). Cohort study of depressive moods in Thai women during late pregnancy and 6-8 weeks of postpartum using the Edinburgh Postnatal Depression Scale (EPDS). *Archives of Women's Mental Health, 9*(3), 131-138.

Liu, E. Y., Koenig, H. G., & Wei, D. (2012). Discovering a blissful island: Religious involvement and happiness in Taiwan. *Sociology of Religion, 73*(1), 46-68.

MacDonald, D. A. (2017). Commentary on "Existential Well-Being: Spirituality or Well-Being?" *Journal of Nervous and Mental Disease*, 205(3): 242-248.

Margolin A, Beitel M, Schuman-Olivier Z, Avants SK (2006). A controlled study of a spiritually-focused intervention for increasing motivation for HIV prevention among drug users. *AIDS Education and Prevention* 18 (4): 311-322

Moon, Y. S., & Kim, D. H. (2013). Association between religiosity/ spirituality and quality of life or depression among living-alone elderly in a South Korean city. *Asia-Pacific Psychiatry* 5(4), 293-300.

Narada, M.T. (1992). *A Manual of Buddhism, Buddha Educational Foundation.* Kuala Lumpur: Buddhist Missionary Society

Nikam, N.A., McKeon, R.P. (editors and translators) (1978). *The Edicts of Asoka.* Chicago, IL: University of Chicago Press

O'Connor, L. E., Berry, J. W., Stiver, D. J., & Rangan, R. K. (2012). Depression, guilt, and Tibetan Buddhism. *Psychology* 3(9), 805-809.

Peltzer, K., Yi, S., & Pengpid, S. (2017). Suicidal behaviors and associated factors among university students in six countries in the Association of Southeast Asian Nations (ASEAN). *Asian Journal of Psychiatry*, 26, 32-38.

Pew Research Center (2008). U.S. Religious Landscape Survey. *The Pew Forum on Religion & Public Life*, p 162-163. Retrieved from: https://www.google.com/url?sa=t&rct=j&q=&esrc=s&source=web &cd=2&ved=0ahUKEwjnroi45oDQAhUa24MKHWoMBxgQFggj MAE&url=http%3A%2F%2Fwww.pewforum.org%2Ffiles%2F2013 %2F05%2Freport-religious-landscape-study- full.pdf&usg=AFQjCNHo6xq96FNYj9DFDNT23soHLK2vpQ&bv m=bv.136811127,d.eWE&cad=rja (accessed on 10/29/16).

Pew Research Center (2012a). Buddhists. Retrieved from: http://www.pewforum.org/2012/12/18/global-religious-landscape- buddhist/ (accessed on 10-27-16).

Pew Research Center (2012b). Asian Americans: A Mosaic of Faiths. Retrieved from: http://www.pewforum.org/2012/07/19/asian- americans-a-mosaic-of-faiths-overview/ (accessed on 10/28/16).

Phillips, R. E., Michelle Cheng, C., Oemig, C., Hietbrink, L., & Vonnegut, E. (2012). Validation of a Buddhist coping measure among primarily non-Asian Buddhists in the United States. *Journal for the Scientific Study of Religion, 51*(1), 156-172.

Rahula A (1974). *What the Buddha Taught.* New York, NY: Grove Press

Ray R (2001). *Secret of the Vajra World.* Boston: Shambhala Meditation Center, p. 13

Religion Facts (2004). Buddhist theism: Is Buddhism theistic or atheistic? Retrieved from http://www.religionfacts.com/theism/buddhism (accessed on 10/28/16)

Rhys Davids, CAF (1971). *Samyutta-Nikaya* (The Book of the Kindred Sayings). London: Luzac publishers, vol I, p 108

Roemer, M. K. (2010a). Religion and psychological distress in Japan. *Social Forces, 89*(2), 559-583.

Roemer, M. K. (2010b). Religion and subjective well-being in Japan. *Review of Religious Research*, 51(4): 411-427

Rungreangkulkij, S., Wongtakee, W. (2008). The psychological impact of Buddhist counseling for patients suffering from symptoms of anxiety. *Archives of Psychiatric Nursing, 22*(3), 127-134

Rungreangkulkij, S., Wongtakee, W., & Thongyot, S. (2011). Buddhist group therapy for diabetes patients with depressive symptoms. *Archives of Psychiatric Nursing, 25*(3), 195-205.

Sachs, E., Rosenfeld, B., Lhewa, D., Rasmussen, A., & Keller, A. (2008). Entering exile: Trauma, mental health, and coping among Tibetan refugees arriving in Dharamsala, India. *Journal of Traumatic Stress, 21*(2), 199-208.

Sahdra, B. K., Shaver, P. R., & Brown, K. W. (2010). A scale to measure nonattachment: A Buddhist complement to Western research on attachment and adaptive functioning. *Journal of Personality Assessment, 92*(2), 116-127.

Saroglou, V., & Dupuis, J. (2006). Being Buddhist in Western Europe: Cognitive needs, prosocial character, and values. *International Journal for the Psychology of Religion, 16*(3), 163-179.

Sayadaw, M. (n.d.) *The Theory of Karma.* Retrieved from: http://www.buddhanet.net/e-learning/karma.htm (accessed on 4/6/17) [note: original source is not given or substantiated]

Schmidt, S. (2011). Mindfulness in east and west–is it the same? In Walach H, Schmdit S, Jonas WB (eds), *Neuroscience, Consciousness and Spirituality* (pp. 23-38). Dordrecht, Netherlands: Springer.

Sethabouppha, H., Kane, C., (2005). Caring for the seriously mentally ill in Thailand: Buddhist family caregiving. *Archives of Psychiatric Nursing, 19*(2), 44-57.

Shiba, K., Nishimoto, M., Sugimoto, M., & Ishikawa, Y. (2015). The Association between Meditation Practice and Job Performance: A Cross-Sectional Study. *PloS one, 10*(5), e0128287.

SLSCR (2007). *Spiritual Life Study of Chinese Residents*, 2007. Dataset downloaded from the Association of Religion Data Archives, www.TheARDA.com. Data were collected by Dr. Anna Sun and her research team and was funded by the John Templeton Foundation (accessed on 11/7/16).

Spijkerman, M. P. J., Pots, W. T. M., & Bohlmeijer, E. T. (2016). Effectiveness of online mindfulness-based interventions in improving mental health: A review and meta-analysis of randomised controlled trials. *Clinical Psychology Review, 45*, 102-114.

Stack, S., & Kposowa, A. J. (2011). Religion and suicide acceptability: A cross-national analysis. *Journal for the Scientific Study of Religion, 50*(2), 289-306.

Tapanya, S., Nicki, R., & Jarusawad, O. (1997). Worry and intrinsic/extrinsic religious orientation among Buddhist (Thai) and Christian (Canadian) elderly persons. *International Journal of Aging and Human Development*, 44, 73-83.

Thanissaro B (1993). *Pañcavaggi Sutta: Five Brethren* (aka: Anatta-lakkhana Sutta: The Discourse on the Not-self Characteristic). Retrieved from http://www.accesstoinsight.org/tipitaka/sn/sn22/sn22.059.than.html (accessed on 2/20/17)

Thanissaro B (1996). *No-self or Not-self?* Retrieved from http://www.accesstoinsight.org/lib/authors/thanissaro/notself2.html (accessed on 11/29/16)

Thanissaro B (2010). *Dhammacakkappavattana Sutta: Setting the Wheel of Dhamma in Motion. Access to Insight* (SN 56.11). Retrieved from: http://www.accesstoinsight.org/tipitaka/sn/sn56/sn56.011.than.html (accessed on 10/25/16)

Thanissaro, P. N. (2011). Measuring attitude towards Buddhism and Sikhism: Internal consistency reliability for two new instruments. *Mental Health, Religion & Culture*, *14*(8), 797-803.

Thaper R (2002). *History of Early India. From Origins to AD1300.* Berkeley: University of California Press

Thera N (2004). *Buddhism and the God-idea.* BuddhaNet (Theraveda Library). Retrieved from http://www.accesstoinsight.org/lib/authors/nyanaponika/godidea.html (accessed on 10/28/16)

Tori, C. D. (1999). Change on psychological scales following Buddhist and Roman Catholic retreats. *Psychological Reports*, *84*(1), 125-126.

Tori, C. D. (2004). Self-representation in a selfless society: reliability and validity of the Tennessee self-concept scale in Thailand. In Shohov SP (ed), *Advances in Psychology Research* 30: 35-56.

Tsuang, M. T., Simpson, J. C. (2008). Commentary on Koenig (2008): "Concerns about measuring 'spirituality' in research". *Journal of Nervous & Mental Disease*, *196*(8), 647-649.

Tzeng, H. M., & Yin, C. Y. (2008). Religious activities of inpatients and their family visitors in Taiwan. *Journal of Holistic Nursing, 26*(2), 98-106.

Vives, S. G., Martin, J. G. A., Trebbau, H., & Aliño, J. L. I. (2011). Meditation and psychosis (P03-31). *European Psychiatry*, *26*, 1200.

Waelde, L. C. (2004). Dissociation and meditation. *Journal of Trauma & Dissociation* 5(2):147-162.

Wang, Z., Koenig H.G., Ma, W., & Liu, L. (2015). Religious Involvement, Suicidal Ideation and Behavior in Mainland China. *International Journal of Psychiatry in Medicine*, *48*(4), 299-316.

Watson B, translator (1993). *The Lotus Sutra*. New York, NY: Columbia University Press, pp 298–303

WCD (2010). *World Christian Database*, 2010. Retrieved from http://www.thearda.com/internationalData/countries/Country_234_2.asp#S_1 (accessed on 11/6/16).

Weaver, A. J., Vane, A., & Flannelly, K. J. (2008). A review of research on Buddhism and health: 1980–2003. *Journal of Health Care Chaplaincy*, *14*(2), 118-132.

Wickrama, K. A. S., Wickrama, K. A. T. (2008). Family context of mental health risk in Tsunami affected mothers: findings from a pilot study in Sri Lanka. *Social Sciences in Medicine*, *66*(4), 994-1007.

Wiist, W. H., Sullivan, B. M., George, D. S., & Wayment, H. A. (2012). Buddhists' religious and health practices. *Journal of Religion and Health*, *51*(1), 132-147.

Wiist, W. H., Sullivan, B. M., Wayment, H. A., & Warren, M. (2010). A web-based survey of the relationship between Buddhist religious practices, health, and psychological characteristics: Research methods and preliminary results. *Journal of Religion and Health*, *49*(1), 18-31.

Williams, P., Tribe, A., Wynne, A. (2012). *Buddhist Thought: A Complete Introduction to the Indian Tradition* (2nd ed). NY, NY: Routledge

Wiltshire, M. G. (1983). The 'suicide' problem in the Pàli Canon. *Journal of the International Association of Buddhist Studies* 6:124-140

Wong, L. C., Chan, E., Tay, S., Lee, K. M., & Back, M. (2010). Complementary and alternative medicine practices among Asian radiotherapy patients. *Asia-Pacific Journal of Clinical Oncology*, *6*(4), 357-363.

Wong, L. P., Fung, H. H., & Jiang, D. (2015). Associations between religiosity and death attitudes: Different between Christians and Buddhists? *Psychology of Religion and Spirituality*, *7*(1), 70-79.

Wongtongkam, N., Ward, P. R., Day, A., & Winefield, A. H. (2014). The influence of protective and risk factors in individual, peer and school domains on Thai adolescents' alcohol and illicit drug use: A survey. *Addictive Behaviors*, *39*(10), 1447-1451.

Woodward FL, translator (1973). *Samyutta-Nikaya* (The Book of the Kindred Sayings). London: Pali Text Society, pp 421-423.

Wuthnow, R., & Cadge, W. (2004). Buddhists and Buddhism in the United States: The scope of influence. *Journal for the Scientific Study of Religion*, *43*(3), 363-380.

WVS (2005-2006). *World Values Survey*, 2005-2006. Dataset was downloaded from the World Values Survey (WORLD VALUES SURVEY Wave 5 2005-2008 OFFICIAL AGGREGATE v.20140429. World Values Survey Association [www.worldvaluessurvey.org]. Aggregate File Producer: Asep/JDS, Madrid SPAIN). Retrieved from http://www.worldvaluessurvey.org/WVSDocumentationWV5.jsp (accessed on 11-7-16)

Xue S, Arya S, Embuldeniya A, Narammalage H, da Silva T, Williams S, Ravindran A (2016). Perceived functional impairment and spirituality/religiosity as predictors of depression in a Sri Lankan spinal cord injury patient population. *Spinal Cord* 54: 1158-1163

Yamaoka, K. (2008). Social capital and health and well-being in East Asia: a population-based study. *Social Science & Medicine*, *66*(4), 885-899.

Yeager, D., Glei, D. A., Au, M., Lin, H.-S., Sloan, R. P., & Weinstein, M. (2006). Religious involvement and health outcomes among older persons in Taiwan. *Social Science & Medicine*, *63*(8), 2228-2241.

Yorston, G. A. (2001). Mania precipitated by meditation: a case report and literature review. *Mental Health, Religion and Culture* 4(2): 209–213

Zhang, J., & Jin, S. (1996). Determinants of suicide ideation: A comparison of Chinese and American college students. <u>Adolescence</u>, 31(122), 451-467.

Zhang, J., Conwell, Y., Zhou, L., & Jiang, C. (2004). Culture, risk factors and suicide in rural China: a psychological autopsy case control study. *Acta Psychiatrica Scandinavica, 110*(6), 430-437.

Zhang, J., Jia, S., Jiang, C., & Sun, J. (2006). Characteristics of Chinese suicide attempters: an emergency room study. *Death Studies, 30*(3), 259-268.

Zhang, J., & Xu, H. (2007). The effects of religion, superstition, and perceived gender inequality on the degree of suicide intent: a study of serious attempters in China. *Omega, 55*(3), 185-197.

Zou, Y., Leung, R., Lin, S., Yang, M., Lu, T., Li, X., Gu, J., Hao, C., Dong, G., & Hao, Y. (2016). Attitudes towards suicide in urban and rural China: a population based, cross-sectional study. *BMC Psychiatry, 16*(1), 162.

ABOUT THE AUTHOR

Harold G. Koenig, M.D., M.H.Sc., completed his undergraduate education at Stanford University, nursing school at San Joaquin Delta College, medical school training at the University of California at San Francisco, and geriatric medicine, psychiatry, and biostatistics training at Duke University Medical Center. He is currently board certified in general psychiatry, and formerly boarded in family medicine, geriatric medicine, and geriatric psychiatry, and is on the faculty at Duke as Professor of Psychiatry and Behavioral Sciences, and Associate Professor of Medicine. He is also Adjunct Professor in the Department of Medicine at King Abdulaziz University, Jeddah, Saudi Arabia, and in the School of Public Health at Ningxia Medical University, Yinchuan, People's Republic of China. Dr. Koenig is Director of the Center for Spirituality, Theology and Health at Duke University Medical Center, and has published extensively in the fields of mental health, geriatrics, and religion, with over 500 scientific peer-reviewed articles and book chapters, and nearly 50 books in print or preparation. His research on religion, health and ethical issues in medicine has been featured on dozens of national and international TV news programs (including ABC's World News Tonight, The Today Show, Good Morning America. Dr. Oz Show, and NBC Nightly News), over a hundred national or international radio programs, and hundreds of newspapers and magazines (including Reader's Digest, Parade Magazine, Newsweek, Time, and Guidepost). Dr. Koenig has given testimony before the U.S. Senate (1998) and U.S. House of Representatives (2008) concerning the benefits of religion and spirituality on public health, and travels widely to give seminars and workshops on this topic. He is the recipient of the 2012 Oskar Pfister Award from the American Psychiatric Association.

www.ingramcontent.com/pod-product-compliance
Lightning Source LLC
Chambersburg PA
CBHW072145280526
45788CB00002B/786